A
Good Angler
in his Time...

Paul Rogers

Grosvenor House
Publishing Limited

This book is published by
Grosvenor House Publishing Ltd
Link House
140 The Broadway, Tolworth, Surrey, KT6 7HT.
www.grosvenorhousepublishing.co.uk

A CIP record for this book
is available from the British Library

ISBN 978-1-83975-649-8

CONTENTS

Book Three - The Barbel Fisher years -
Waiting for the Reel to Scream

PREFACE

Writing a book - how difficult can that be?

Having written articles for angling magazines, a book seemed like a good idea. Twenty-plus articles make a whole, or so I thought. Interconnecting in the passing of life, from child, through adult into a later maturity, time did not flow as smoothly as I would have wished.

Within their pages, chapters swell and fall through years and the emotions the writer felt, good times and bad, with omissions that had not made the grade or were simply too personal for inclusion.

The book will not be filled with big fish, the essence arises from a place of growth and development; the catches contained within give illustration to the picture of a story.

A path often travelled by an angler and man, a road less acknowledged.

ACKNOWLEDGEMENTS

In 1994, the first article I wrote for a magazine had been encouraged by a better angler than myself being approached by the editor of a carp magazine, who needed contributors. He suggested me, and I wrote three articles before I ran out of photographic evidence to illustrate each piece.

Forward seventeen years. I joined the Barbel Society with little thought of writing an article for the magazine 'Barbel Fisher'; however, the idea of having something in print after all those years enlightened the writer within. Now in 2021, a decade later, only one issue has not included an article of mine within its pages. The satisfaction and joy felt seeing my written word every six months lifts my spirit and soul. When depression sneaks up on me, as it does, the cathartic healing of pressing the keys on the computer acts as a medicine.

All the chapters in book three, apart from the last two, first saw the light of day in a 'Barbel Fisher' magazine. I must acknowledge the thanks and encouragement of all the editors who have come and gone in that time, especially Chris Jones, who has been a friend and mentor in prompting a better standard of work from me. Another acknowledgement must go to Steve Pope. We do not always see eye-to-eye about the subject matter, yet he stays neutral and allows the article to be included. Each of these articles has been altered to make them more book-ready, and to insert the correct tense, past to present, to provide a better introduction to the issue described.

During the last two years, I have been asked to write a chapter for other books, and for that, and the encouragement, I must thank Terry Theobald, a friend and author I look up to. For approaching me to write that first article in 1994, Paul

Klinkenborg gets the credit; without him and his proofreading work on this and the early work, none of this would have happened.

The acknowledgements that need to be included though, are the most important:

Marie, my wife for twenty-four years, who I love, and to whom I am thankful for her support for me. Without her, there would have been no balance in my life – not to mention the encouragement she has given to bring this book to fruition.

Chris Rogers, my stepfather, for his patience and time when he encouraged me, and took me fishing, for the lessons he taught me that stood me in good stead throughout life, to appreciate the wildlife around us, and to treat every man fairly. Sadly missed, passing in 1991.

My mother. A rock in times of trouble. Whatever I may have done, she has stood by me, loving me throughout.

My brother Jeff, who has through thick and thin been patient with me, and has carried on fishing with me, even during the years when I drifted into depression.

My brother Dave for his artwork for this book. His work has been displayed in galleries, and he is much respected as a portrait artist. See his website; if you search Google his site is top of the list. David Weekes, artist.

Kevan Scripps, a childhood friend who, with his dad, lit the spark to fish, taking me on coach trips with their small fishing club when I was not the easiest boy to have around. Sadly, we have lost contact again; I would like to meet up one day.

Stuart Richardson, a non-biased friend, who does not mince his words. He has read the book before proofreading, and he told me in no uncertain terms that if he did not like it, it would be put down in the first couple of pages. Well, he completed the reading, and gave constructive criticism that I acted upon to make the book a better read for you.

Thank You All.

THE CATALYST

Walking into the Aladdin's cave that is a fishing tackle shop, somewhere in a small provincial town in Berkshire, residing in a run-down shopping precinct, past its prime, the angler looks about him, his sole purpose to buy a few oddments needed to restock his tackle bag, and needing to return to work, his lunch break nowhere long enough.

All appears quiet; muffled sounds could be heard, way out back in the stock room, most likely the owner riddling maggots and caster for bait. Slowly, the angler gazes around him and locates the shelves with the items he wishes to buy. Unnoticed, two other men have approached the front door, making him aware of their presence as the chime rings with the opening of the door.

There was no recognition between the three; just a greeting, however, a nod and an impersonal 'Hello'. As so often happens, though, a conversation started; the two anglers openly declared their obsession with carp fishing, their chat fed by the requirement to wheelbarrow everything but the kitchen sink to their chosen swims, or to fish as close as possible to their parked car! The first angler had a different mindset; he discussed with them his preference to arrive with just a small bag of tackle, a little bait, and, if weather allowed, not even an umbrella!

Meanwhile, the tackle shop owner appeared from the rear of the shop and joined in the conversation. However, the angler remembered he should be back at work - he was already five minutes late. He put the items of tackle on the counter, and after the owner had cashed his money, hurriedly left the shop.

The following day

Having forgotten something on his previous visit the shop, he made a detour to the shop once more between calls for work. Today, the owner was out front, sitting at the counter, and offered him a cup of coffee, which was gratefully accepted. They whiled away the time available in conversation that returned to the one from the day before.

A smile came upon the shop-owner's face as he recounted how the conversation yesterday had continued. He related how the other anglers had recognised the first angler! He was bemused, and asked what they had said. The owner replied that the two anglers had asked him in hushed tones: "Do you know who that was?" He had no idea and asked them to tell him. **"That was 'Creeping Jesus' – he used to be a good angler in his time"**.

The angler is me. My response required a calming of feelings; being told you used to be good is not what you want to hear! It had been twenty-plus years since that name had been given to me, and I had now left the carp fishing on the Colne Valley to seek pastures new. The comment was a kick in the teeth, spurring me back on the path of obsession once again.

In these pages, the story, a path of conquest, an obsession and how in later life it turned on itself, grew, was fed, going through famine and time of plenty. Seeing fishing as a healer, and a cathartic release from the need to achieve. It will recall records of special days' fishing, the ups and downs of how obsession takes hold of a man. From the early years, how the seed was dug into the ground of childhood, being fed in teenage years to bring about germination. The growing into a plant, the transition in the confusion of early adulthood; flowering, taking on the responsibility of family life, pruning and looking back from a mature outlook in retirement.

The personal journey, taking in the life outside of angling as much as the life within. Consumed in actions of selfishness that a sport can bring upon a man, it is forgotten how the opposites are on a collision course, each vying for our time and complete life. The story of how life outside of angling shaped the path from childhood through manhood, and the twists and turns created, shows a road more travelled, walked and run by many men seeking an identity in their quest. There is joy, sadness, excitement, hurt and pain; but through it all, though, a life empathised with, even if not acknowledged.

ENJOY.

BOOK ONE

Childhood -
Sowing the seed

CHAPTER ONE

CHILDHOOD - SOWING THE SEED

Most memories fade into the mists of time, becoming discoloured as an old photograph turns yellow with age, disappearing into a memory bank overloaded with a life of events and people. Some, however, burn into the fabric of our souls, scarring our spirit, remaining on the hard drive deep within us. These create the heart of who we are, continuing to resurface if distractions have led us away.

As a child, are we aware, having a knowledge or an understanding of obsession? The mystical tangle of a spell cast upon an individual, which draws us away from reality, pulling us into fantastical, whimsical delusion of a goal that is unobtainable while it drifts forever further away from us; goalposts move as it tempts us with ever increasingly impossible achievement. For an angler, the record weight we had been chasing for years is broken by another angler, and we are driven on by the quest to reach the next 'Holy Grail'....

The first time a fishing rod or net is picked up, can we grasp the magnitude of the action? Was the choice our own, or had the rod/net been given to us by another person, who also had no power over the life it would change? My first memory of fishing held all the innocence a child needs; using a rod, bought from Woolworth's, the go-to shop of the day (1965) as part of a kit, consisting of a three-foot rod, a small, round reel loaded with string-like catgut, a grayling-bob float, and what could only be described as a bent pin for a hook. The rod, if that what it could be called, was similar to some rods of the day, which were reputedly made from tank aerials! It appeared to be a fine,

bendy metal stick about three feet in length, onto which the reel had been bound with cotton, six inches from the bottom. There was only the single eye whipped to the opposite end. However, fish were caught from the bottom of my grandparents' garden; giant gudgeon from the River Thames at Henley, where they had moved that year.

The family had travelled in my father's old Ford Popular car from Harlow New Town to visit my mother's parents, who had left Bow in London to live in a small bungalow built in the garden of her older sister and her husband. It was the furthest we had travelled from home; excitement filled us and buoyed our spirits. The fishing rod had been brought a couple of days earlier, while shopping with dad and my elder brother, Dave. Neither of us, as I remember, showed any excitement; it would not be until the day the fishing took place that we would bathe in the thrill. Planned activities and days out had been cancelled at the last moment far too often in our early lives; it was difficult to believe until we saw.

The sun shone down on the two brothers, sitting dangling their feet into the water, holding a rod each; excitement rose, disguising their lack of fishing ability. The tackle was totally useless; unable to cast, we gave up trying to fish more than inches off the rod-tip in eighteen inches of water, yet fish still tried to pull the oversized float across the surface. I don't know who had dug the worms from the garden which were used as bait, but I do remember the looks of disgust on my dad's face as he tried to put them on the hook. I recall that I must have been a natural, taking to impaling them with glee.

To a young boy's eyes, the gudgeon which hooked themselves were giants; in those times, though, their size would dwarf any caught by anglers in the twenty-first century. None of them were less than four inches long, and most were nearer five or six; their colourful markings left an image on my mind's eye, remembered to be drawn on a year later, as the day was not to be repeated until a school-friend encouraged me to join him fishing a small local pond.

The summer of 1965 drifted by; the memories seem to have been lost in the hazy mist of time, protecting me from the hurt and pain of the broken home life, which we experienced as a family. An occasional glimpse of joy, building go-carts and riding them down the steep cycle- paths that led to the town shopping centre; coming home with grazed knees and torn clothes; spending time with friends, spending as much time away from home as possible.

Somewhere around this time, one of my friends, Kevan Scripps, talked to me about his pastime called fishing. Both he and his dad Ron belonged to a small fishing club, Newman and Guardia; affiliated to the London Anglers' Association, going on fortnightly coach trips; Kevan introduced me first to a small pond on the other side of town, which everyone called the 'Hospital Pond', simply as it was close to the hospital!

It was situated amongst a copse, shaded from the sun, and had become heavily silted, giving off that stale stench of years of decomposing vegetation rotting on the bottom; our young noses were not put off, though - we were having too much fun. To get there, we would ride our push-bikes, old and rusty as they were, we did not care - it seemed that all of the families we knew had similar bikes, no one batted an eyelid about being poor.

All of us had moved, willingly or not, from the slums of London, deluded by the government's promise of a better life in the country; well, in a new town, away from the smog and old derelict bomb sites remaining in London twenty years after the end of World War Two.

The rod, brought for me the year before, was soon discarded; however, Kevan lent me an old rod his dad had disregarded for a more modern 12' fibreglass rod - a Hardy Matchmaker, if my memory serves me correctly - ten feet of greenheart that had a replacement top section of early fibreglass. The rod weighed a ton to a young, weak, sickly lad like me, but it enabled me to look the part; with a 'Intrepid Black Prince' fixed-spool reel sitting on the dirty cork handle, loaded with proper monofilament line, I was a 'real' fisherman. Interestingly, the rod came as a gift from Kevan's dad, and this tackle sufficed for at least three or four more years.

The pond was covered by beds of lilies; reeds covered much of the margin, and if we arrived early in the morning, ripples of fish swirling or bubbling in the deep silt, a layer deeper than the depth of water above it, could be witnessed. Our first attempts at fishing soon saw fish being caught; however, using worm as bait, we caught several at a time; a population of three-spined sticklebacks, as numerous as they were, appeared to be the primary species, but a change of bait brought a change in fortune.

We watched the older boys fishing nearby; they all caught bigger fish than us, fish called tench and crucian carp. To our eyes they were big fish, but as with the sticklebacks, the biomass appeared to be too high, which stunted their growth; never in the year or so that we fished there did we see either at a weight of more than about 8oz. In all the years that have passed since then, I have only witnessed either tench or crucian carp so small in a group of gravel pits in Cambridgeshire, a story for the later chapters. The bait that successfully caught these fish for the older boys was good old 'Mother's Pride' bread, by its correct name; nowadays, it's more likely to be 'Warburtons'!

The Hospital Pond was where I learnt to fish the 'Lift Method', using peacock quills cut into lengths of two or three inches, attached by a float rubber, with a split-shot, usually a BB or AAA, two inches from the hook. The shot would submerge the float, being too heavy, so we would set it over-depth and tighten the line to make the float cock upright in the surface film of the pond. The bread-flake was folded over the hook and pressed lightly before casting a rod-length out onto the edge of the lilies. As there were so many fish in the pond, hunger drove them to feed avidly all day long, so after casting, a float would not rest for more than a minute; it would bob crazily before either lying flat or sliding under. However, just because the float indicated a fish had taken the bait, it did not always result in a hooked fish. For every twenty bites, we would be lucky if we hooked just one;

I suspect now that most of the fish were too small to mouth the size of bait we dangled in front of them, and it was only when a slightly larger specimen picked up the bread that we would succeed - this would include fish of an ounce and above, while a fish of 8oz was a rare thing.

The 'lift method' was not used by design; it was stumbled upon by accident. Well, not having any spare money to spend on tackle, split-shot and floats were in short supply. The floats we used were cut-down lengths of peacock quill, bought from the fishing tackle shop, as short as two inches, so we could get as many as possible from each twelve-inch quill. The shot was just the one on the line, again because the pot of assorted shot purchased would need to last as long as we could make it.

It wasn't until a few years later that we learnt of the method as one used by 'proper' anglers while watching the only television show of the day that had a fishing segment, 'Out of Town' with Jack Hargreaves, one week covering float-fishing for tench.

After coming home from church on Sunday morning - a routine followed religiously every week; I had to attend because mum played the church organ - I would sit down in front of the TV to watch Jack show the general viewing population the life of a countryman. Not only did he go fishing, but he would cook the fish, too; he would go on game shoots, collect Norfolk reed to thatch houses... a true man of the country, with a life a boy like me dreamed of.

A film released around the same time also shaped my life; 'A Ring of Bright Water' gave birth to my dream of living on a croft, a small-holding in the Scottish Highlands, far away from the hustle and bustle of town/city living. Being self-sufficient, growing my own crops, having a pet otter who caught sea-trout for dinner - childhood enlightenment fuelling the embers of early obsession.

CHAPTER TWO

THE COACH TRIPS - A SPROUTING SEED

By the start of 1966, with a few paddies (tantrums) thrown to get my way, mum and dad agreed to let me go fishing with Kevan and his dad's club on their fortnightly coach trips. I have doubts as to whether it was to keep me happy; more likely so they could have some peace for a day, even if it meant waking up at the unearthly time of 3.30am to make sure I caught the coach! The trips always fell on a Sunday, which gave me another excuse not to attend church, too - if not in Sunday school, I would be forced to sit with mum playing the organ; she thought I enjoyed pulling the levers and knobs for her, but I will now admit it was done to make time pass more quickly.

The first trip, at the end of January, nearly put me off going ever again. The weather was terrible, and without suitable clothing and an umbrella, the cold, wet rain that lasted for most the time fishing dampened my spirits. To top it all, no one caught a single fish on the windswept Ten Mile Bank on the River Great Ouse near Ely in Cambridgeshire. Arriving home soaking wet and dirty, mum threw a paddy of her own - she had to wash my clothes on her day of rest and serve up a dinner, warmed up over a pan of boiling water on the hob. Oh, how a memory like this reminds of how old I have become; a decade later, we were warming the food in a microwave.

I didn't think that my parents would agree to me going on another trip on the club coach; however, my delight could not be hidden two weeks later when waking at 3.45am to go adventuring again. I have a vague memory of many of these jaunts, which lasted a couple of years; a few, though, do stand out.

Winning the Fur and Feather - December 1967

The trip before Christmas 1967, we travelled up to St. Benet's Abbey on the River Bure in Norfolk; unfortunately, as this coincided with a flood tide, everything was muddy and wet, like that first trip eleven months before. It was impossible to fish more than a few feet from the bank; the tackle we all used was totally useless in such powerful, flowing water, all being used to fishing the Rivers Lea or Stort closer to home. However, baits dropped close in produced some small roach and skimmer bream, and being fortunate to be fishing in a bay, I weighed in over a pound of them to win the match.

Arriving home with a food hamper so big it took three of us to carry in made me the hero of the month. Mum and dad had saved up for Christmas, but the turkey, and all the other goodies, meant the family had its best Christmas ever.

Hartford Marina. Huntington, Great Ouse - A fantastic catch of roach - March 1967

The weather was unusually warm for the time of year; the temperature and sunny conditions were more akin to late

April/early May, being a balmy 15 degrees C. On arrival, as happened every trip, all the anglers, after paying a shilling, drew numbered pieces of paper out of a cloth bag to choose their swim. The lower the number you picked gave you a better choice; my number was not particularly low, so I walked off in the middle of the stream of eager fishermen on the bank, all wanting to get the best peg, meaning a better chance to win the money from the draw-bag.

My reason for picking the chosen swim was unknown; in those days, watercraft played little part in how or where I fished - all I remember is it being a nice sunny, warm swim with the light breeze blowing off my back; Kevan had taken the next swim to my left. As I had not really mastered the art of legering yet, float-fishing was my only option; I did enjoy watching a float, though, and these conditions favoured the presentation it would achieve.

Bait consisted of a pint of white maggots costing a mere shilling (5p in decimal currency) and a pint of hemp, while some slices of bread (not actually needed) had also been dropped into my basket. Fishing was restricted by how far I was able to catapult the loose feed; on this particular day it was possible to reach twenty - twenty-five feet out, giving me five feet of water to fish in.

In those days, and for a few more years, all matches were fished to size-limits. The LAA (London Anglers' Association) set their own, based on those standardised by the local Water Boards. It would be many years before the Environment Agency became the controlling national body; in 1968, we would have to purchase a licence for every region we travelled to fish in. The smaller the species of fish, the smaller the standard would be; gudgeon and bleak needed to be five inches from nose to fork of the tail, dace seven, roach and rudd eight, while bream and chub needed to be a foot (twelve inches), before they could be weighed in.

It was only ten minutes after the starting whistle (matches would be started in this manner, and finish at a predestined time) when my float slipped under the still surface of the marina. A strike connected with a silvery roach, quickly retrieved to a waiting hand. Measured on the ruler laid out on the side of my basket, it sickeningly only reached seven-and-a-half inches. Thinking that as I had caught so early, more would be caught, I wetted my keepnet, a terrible thing we would not use now - six feet long and eighteen inches in diameter, made of coarse, knotted string like gut - and slid the roach inside to await the expected company.

As the day wore on, I amassed a huge - for a young lad - catch of over fifty roach; unfortunately, however, all were like peas in a pod and none were over eight inches, however much I tried to stretch them! There would have been more, but a shoal of pike terrorised the roach as I was winding them in; ten or more were lost to attacks as the fish were being brought to the bank.

Kevan, in the next swim, with a better tackle armoury, tackled up a heavier rod, with a pike-bung as a float, and a shop-bought snap-tackle (two treble hooks on a wire trace) on which one of the roach from my net was impaled. Within minutes, the bung was being pulled across the water, before Kevan set the hooks into a double-figure pike, which thrashed the water in front of us as he netted it. Again, due to the way things were done then, an unsuitable method of unhooking - now banned - was used: a gag was used to force the fish's mouth open, and the hooks were removed with no finesse, causing blood to flow. Looking back in disdain, it is not possible to right the wrongs we did then, but it is right that we never return to such barbaric behaviour.

The time to stop fishing had been set for 3.30pm. Kevan had landed five pike, all high-single or low-doubles in weight. I had approximately fifty roach still in the net, which would not be weighed, as none were over eight inches. We guesstimated a total of about ten or eleven pounds - this was the biggest catch I had made, and even though a single bream won the match, I knew I had really been the winner.

Bures Lake and Suffolk Stour - November 1967 - Giant ruffe

1967 was a strange year for weather; the spring had been warm and dry, the late summer/autumn was bathed in an Indian summer filled with sunny, still days. Childhood memories can be clouded; the truth may be seen differently - however, that is how it is remembered, empowering positive thoughts, away from the turmoil at home. As the family fractured, mum and dad distanced themselves from each other, and their separation was not far off.

The two-hour coach journey from Harlow in Essex to the intended venue, Bures Lake, was filled with fishing talk, as on every trip the club made. Discussion took place of how we would fish the lake and what we expected to catch – tench, which the lake was famed for at that time.

First view of the lake was one of beauty; a low mist drifted over the lake and surrounding fields, inspiring childhood imagination with thoughts of ghosts floating within it. The sun, though, had other ideas, warming the mist as it rose; everything was soon lit by the low autumnal glow, and we approached the lake through the dewy grass.

Unlike other trips, the rush for swims seemed to take place in silence, no one wishing to break the spell. Each angler settled quietly into their chosen spot, slowly tackling up, most with the standard lift method, including myself, but the more skilled and mature were using a swing-tip and were legering further out in the lake.

Swing-tips were a wonderful bite indicator; on lakes, Fenland drains or canals they worked perfectly, but they were no use on flowing water, as we found out through trial and error later in the weirpool at Dobbs Weir on the River Lea closer to home. They hung from the rod-tip, the angler would tension the line until the tip would move slightly forward, and on the bite the tip either moved forward or dropped back as a fish mouthed the bait. If there was a flow, the tip would be pulled up to an angle that made it worthless; if a fish took the bait, it would be the rod moving, the swing-tip not having any scope for movement left.

I was sitting with hushed silence surrounding me, hidden in a reed-bed, the float cast a rod-length out, semi-cocked against a single swan-shot, a piece of bread-flake on the size 12 Au Lion d'Or hook to 3lb nylon. Unfortunately, the tench were under the mist's spell, and as the sun rose not a fish was caught; everyone became restless, some even looking at the river that ran besides the lake. As no other anglers from another club were present, the club chairman took the decision to allow those who wished to go and try the river.

Being an impatient young man, my tackle was hastily moved across to a nice-looking swim on the river. The flow was not that strong, so the tackle set up stayed the same. Only the bait was changed to a lobworm; however, the fish in the river seemed not to be interested, either. Mid- afternoon, lying in the grass half asleep, watching the float out of the corner of my eye - my enthusiasm had waned hours before - I noticed the float moving differently to any movement throughout the day. It didn't go under the water's surface, or lie flat, but drifted from side to side, rocking gently. Picking up the rod, I was surprised to feel some tension - something had taken my bait! It swung to my hand without any resistance; not recognising it, I wondered what this ugly fish was... It looked like a perch that had been washed and lost its stripes; its skin was mottled, and its double dorsal fin was raised in anger at being pulled from its watery home.

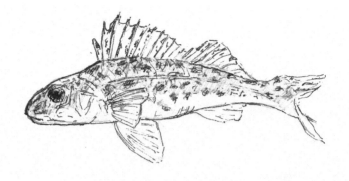

I called over the nearest fisherman, who identified it as a ruffe; he also informed me it was way over the required size limit, too. Ruffe needed to be over five inches, and this specimen was over eight! It was placed in the keepnet to be weighed in at the end of the day. In those days, the obsession of angling had not taken hold; taking part was only for fun, and breaking records was not on my radar, so when the ruffe was recorded as 3.75oz, it was returned to the river with little thought. It wasn't important that I didn't return the highest weight of the day, either.

It was not until reading my copy of the Angling Times a few weeks later, when the record table was published, that I saw it had equalled the record for a ruffe, but it was water under the bridge.

CHAPTER THREE

THE SEED TAKES ROOT

Come 14th March 1968, as every year, the fishing season came to an end. It was not until 1986, when the government changed the law to allow fishing on stillwaters, that fishing for coarse fish was allowed all year round; even then, it was on the premise that we were bait-fishing for stocked trout in the three months between March 14th and June 16th. Many of us living near London fished Farlows Lake on the Boyer's ticket, using boilies for trout! Canals were opened up later, and rivers are still closed; however, in 1968, March saw a three-month furlough enforced upon us.

Fishing was starting to get its hook into my life. At ten years old and a bit, my need for independence grew, and I wanted to be seen as a grown-up and able to look after myself. My father had, by this time, left the family home; however, we still saw him on occasional visits. He now lived just down the road from the Hospital Pond, and visits would include me slipping away for a few hours to catch small crucian and tench.

Mum had started work at Sainsbury's depot in Hoddesdon, and her fledgling relationship with Chris, our stepfather, was to develop soon after. I cannot remember the first time he came home to meet us; however, my first impressions saw a man in contrast to my dad - he was fun to be around, always willing to talk and help, and he also displayed a mind which sought knowledge. He built his own fishing tackle and some home furnishing, a complete music centre in a beautiful wooden cabinet that took pride of place in the living room.

By June 1968, with a more suitable push-bike to ride, the River Stort and backwaters on the far side of Harlow were

accessible; carrying my basket across my shoulder with the rod tied to the crossbar, days would be spent seeking out fish of all species. On the River Stort, if things became boring, there was a large head of native crayfish, sadly now almost extinct, having succumbed to the virus brought in by the American Signal Crayfish that came to the country to feed hungry diners in restaurants. The European crayfish were small and brown, and they willingly would take a maggot or lobworm when fish were hard to come by. If fishing with a friend, a match would be held to see who could catch the most.

However, the fish that took precedence most days were the proud, stripy perch, who lived by a sunken car under the road bridge near the train station. Many a day was spent lingering under the bridge; even if it was raining, shelter was found there until it was dry enough to ride home. None of these perch grew much bigger than 12oz or so; however, we would catch up to ten a day.

I soon grew tired of this spot, however - it was crowded most days, with maybe five or six young lads fishing - so solitude was sought elsewhere. Cycling up onto the A414, the road that travelled from Bishops Stortford and beyond to the east and

St Albans to the west, a small backwater was found, overgrown and appearing little fished. The first time a line was cast, the lobworm bait was taken by a different species, not the intended perch. To my dismay, it fell off the hook as it was drawn towards my little landing net, and a roach estimated at over a pound slipped back from the net's rim, never to be seen again. Nothing was ever landed or hooked from that spot again, not for the lack of trying, so I soon moved on. Further along the main road, a small side road led to a ford crossing the backwater further downstream, where more exciting swims appeared, crying out to be fished. Over the next couple of months, plenty of perch were landed to over a pound in weight - and another species came to my attention.

A shoal of chub patrolled along the backwater; around fifty fish approaching two or three pounds each would swim past every day. It was never discovered where they fed' none were ever caught, but one day I witnessed an ambush that still stays imprinted vividly upon my soul. If fishing on the double bend a hundred yards below the ford, the chub would pass at 4.00pm every day, almost to the minute. At each pass here, the shoal became agitated, speeding up to escape something unseen.

On this particular day, the sun was up; the fishing was poor, so a decision to sit and watch the shoal go by seemed a good one. As they swam past, half of them already upstream of me, a massive log-shaped image came shooting out from the tangled roots of the bush on the opposite bank. The stream was only fifteen feet wide at this point and about three feet deep, which meant this apparition was less than ten feet away - a pike of, for this watercourse, immense proportions grabbed a chub across the flank and turned tail into its lair. To a young mind, this fish was a giant, and I guessed at a length of over forty inches; however, it was observed that its girth was thin, and that would have kept the weight down to less than 20lb, but it was still a big fish etched upon the window of my soul.

During this year, the family relationships metamorphosed, with Chris becoming a bigger part of our lives. His visits in the evenings and at weekends became accepted by the children, and we took to him, enjoying having him around. He made mum happier, making our lives more bearable too. The change in emotional charge in the family gave the release to be free to enjoy ourselves as children - the older brothers became more confident to spend more time away from home, in my case fishing and in Dave's growing up - his story is his own, not for inclusion here.

The fishing started to take me further away from home, riding the bike along the River Stort's towpaths as far as Roydon downstream, where both the old course of the River Stort and the Navigation flowing to the River Lea provided an opportunity to fish elsewhere. A distraction, however, interested me more. Another smaller backstream, halfway there, held a shoal of chub, much bigger than those seen in the stream I had fished before. It was here that I learnt the art of floating a crust on the flow, under overhanging branches, to the spot where a chub would be lying. Free-lined lobworm also brought results, yet it wasn't as much fun as watching the crust disappear in a small vortex and the line tightening along the water surface, before striking into a chub that tried to get back into the weed or roots.

Earlier in the year, a Samson spring balance had been purchased from the local fishing-tackle-cum-pet shop. It wasn't very reliable, or accurate, weighing in divisions of two ounces to a limit of eight pounds; it had yet to be pulled to that extent, nothing bigger than a pound had worried me until these chub. The smallest caught from the stream weighed 2lb 4oz; the largest a heady 3lb 12oz. They may have weighed more, or less; it wasn't important, as the need to chase the biggest or the most still had not raised its head above the parapet.

The rod used was still the greenheart fibreglass-tipped one that had been given to me by Kevan's dad. It wasn't suited to fishing in this manner; its action could have been called tippy, having no bend in the lower two sections of greenheart; the fibreglass didn't give much movement, either - given how little it did, in hindsight it surprises me that I ever hooked a single fish at all.

It would be two more years later, during a visit to Simpsons of Turnford, a renowned tackle shop, that an Avon rod blank came to be in my possession. Buying a set of eyes and whipping nylon, a cork handle and sliding reel-guides, an attempt was made to make my first rod! It could never be said that the Avon rod looked as good as one bought from a shop: the eyes had been whipped with no finesse; it looked rough and ready, varnished with a thick, heavy coating, and many another angler must have laughed at it over the decade it was on show while fishing on the Lea and on the trips to fish the Lagoons at Broxbourne with Chris; however, it did the job asked of it, and is still looked back on with joy.

CHAPTER FOUR

WITNESSING GIANTS –
THE SEED METAMORPHOSED

As mum and Chris developed their relationship over the months, 1968 became 1969, and Chris had started taking me fishing. He had a ticket to fish the Lagoons at Broxbourne in Hertfordshire, which were controlled by Hall's Angling Scheme, the forerunner to Cemex, who controlled a lot of gravel pits and rivers available to fish in the south of England. A venue book of the time records much smaller fish than now: Wraysbury One, the gravel pit, home to Mary, a carp who held the British record several times in the 1990s-2000s, had only a 13lb 12oz carp shown as its best ...!

We always fished the North Lagoon, the nearest to the River Lea as it run from Dobbs Weir into the Crown Fishery. The Lagoon, to a young lad, was an ocean, covering over one hundred and twenty acres; the main body had two smaller bodies of water joined by narrow channels and a small cutting, accessed off the towpath of the Crown Fishery about a hundred yards long and fifteen yards wide.

The water in the Lagoon was gin-clear, full of weed, and after a short marginal slope it dropped down to up to twenty feet or more. Having been dug in the late 1940s, the bottom was uneven, and gravel bars were evident, coming up to less than eight feet. To an angler like Chris, these were seen as fish-catching spots, as he proved time and again. Locating them was not always simple; at that time, the practice of plumbing with a marker rod wasn't regularly seen. In those days we didn't own bait-boats and echo-sounders; the only depth-finding method we knew was a plummet on float tackle, but this only worked at relatively short distances, so most of the water was a mystery. Old knowledge informed us that counting a leger down, a second for every foot, gives some idea, and this was done; ironically, after many years, it is found to be reasonably accurate!

Tench to make the eyes water

On the first visits to the water, perch would find a lobworm float-fished in the margins; only small samples were caught, but we were happy to catch anything. We would arrive early in the morning, getting to the bankside at dawn; every time, tench were seen patrolling the margin slope, and their size took our breath away. These were not small specimens as seen at the Hospital Pond in the past - these were true giants. Even Chris, an experienced fisherman, was flabbergasted; he believed they were all over 5lb in weight - maybe much more. The British record at the time was 8lb 8oz, and having caught fish of that size since, it would not be hard to believe that some of these tench were at least large enough to threaten the then record. Never did we see more than two at any time; more likely, they swam past individually. The best place to observe them was in the narrow cut as they swam out or in at the entrance. We did see them occasionally in the large bay further down the bank, but as hard as we might try, not one graced the bank.

As autumn approached, I was armed with my new rod, with a screw-in top eye to mount a swing-tip, while Chris taught me how to fish for bream, with a small Arlesey bomb and a hooklength of two feet to a size ten hook. Bread or a bunch of maggots would be cast over a spot we had pre-baited with bread-crumb groundbait the night before caught me my first bream of 2lb 8oz, lifting the swing-tip a couple of inches up from the surface to show a bite.

Those Sunday morning fishing trips with Chris are remembered not just for the fishing. Every time we went, Chris would come into the bedroom to wake me up, whispering: "Be quiet, we mustn't wake your mum"; we would creep downstairs, going into the kitchen to see he had already made a flask and sandwiches. I would quickly eat a bowl of cereal, being told if I did not eat, we would not go.

The tackle was by the front door, from which we tip-toed out and loaded Chris's car. The little Hillman Imp, which a year later took the whole family (five of us) and enough luggage on a fortnight's holiday to the Lake District and Scotland - how it did it will never be known – was powered by a 600cc engine; no way was it strong enough, lacking the torque to be driven over mountain passes, yet it did us proud.

On return home, usually about 1.00pm, in time for a roast dinner, mum would put on an over-acted drama of pretending she had not known where we had been - it would have been more realistic if she didn't have a broad smile upon her face. The facade was kept up through the years, and became part of the ritual that was fishing - it still shines brightly in my memory bank.

Chris's Pike, a record fish if ever there was!

February 1970

Chris would spend most fishing trips in the winter fishing a sink-and-draw sprat or plug for pike on the Lagoon. The normal run of fish would be considered jacks, all single- figure fish up to about 8lb; there were rumours of much larger fish present in the lagoons, yet no reports of one being landed had been heard in recent years.

On the day in question, we left the house around 7.00am, on a cold freezing morning; fine frost covered the ground, and Chris drove slower than usual to ensure a safe arrival at the lake. Following the track down to the river - known so well, it could be travelled with our eyes closed, the journey was undertaken so frequently - the bottom of Meadgate Lane was soon reached.

Turning right at the river, we headed towards the path that went between the prefab houses up to the Lagoon. These prefabs had been built after the Second World War to house families who had been bombed out of London during the Blitz. It was surprising they were still in use, as many looked rusty and about to fall apart, but the families living in them considered them home. However, as time moved on, all would be bull-dozed and modern bungalows would replace them. This path was pitted and full of ruts, a danger to any loose fittings under the car; even exhausts fell victim, as witnessed by the odd one lying at the side of the path. Turning left, a short drive of fifty yards found us behind the corner of the bay where we fished for the perch.

A strong breeze blew from the North-West, and grey clouds scudded across the sky, threatening rain later. Looking out over the Lagoon, Chris had the air of a man on a mission; the sense of purpose felt tangible, as though even I could feel the sixth sense he bathed in - a feeling I have felt many times since; however, for myself, not an aura from another individual. It was dismissed; the belief in magical, mystical awareness did not exist... did it?

The tackle Chris set up was special. Years before, he had made a Dick Walker Mark IV Carp rod - from the splitting of the bamboo cane, to shaping the handle, he had done it all; a rod worthy to catch a monster if ever there was one. The reel was an intrepid Deluxe loaded with 12lb Maxima line.

Not only was the rod self-made: the float used was a home-made Dennis Pye model made from twelve inches of Indian reed with a pilot float glued to it a couple of inches from each end. The design was made to lie flat on the surface as a bite indicator. Before the trace was attached, a 1oz leger was put on the line, followed by another home-made item, the eighteen-inch trace consisting of a size 6 single hook and size 10 treble below it.

Our bait for the day was sprats brought from the fishmonger's the day before. Each one was over six inches long, more like a small herring; not like those sold today, which are usually only three or four inches if you are lucky. One was hooked lightly on the trace, and to enable him to get the bait out to the required feature – a gravel bar found on a previous trip - a balloon was blown up halfway and attached to the leger with a piece of bent wire. The bait was lowered into the water at the rod-tip, and the wind quickly would propel the balloon and tackle outward. Once over the desired spot, a sharp pull released the lead and bait to the bottom. The balloon would drift away to the horizon, never to be seen again - we were not so conscious of leaving rubbish as we are now. The gods were with us that day, and the first attempt had the bait positioned forty yards out alongside the bar in question.

While waiting for action, I spent time using sink-and-draw a short way up the bank. Time past slowly, and after two hours boredom started to set in. Walking up to Chris, I saw movement; he lifted the rod, and let the bail-arm release line before winding down to strike. The rod took on an alarming battle-curve, and the line started to sing in the wind - that eerie howling of a line tensioned to its limit.

Watching the rod-tip, it could be seen flexing, and being moved by an unseen force. Chris didn't say a word; a picture of concentration, coiled like a spring, tension seen on the lines of his face. For ten minutes nothing appeared to change, but then disaster struck: Chris must have been aware before it happened, as I had seen him fidgeting with the reel-fitting, but I didn't take any notice until the reel fell off the rod-handle and crashed onto the hard ground.

Without saying a word Chris bent down and - not as I expected - released the bail-arm of the reel and started to play the fish by hand! The battle continued for about another ten minutes, and even with this handicap Chris got the upper hand. However, a new problem arose: the fish was now lying in the margin, tired and ready to be netted, but the landing net, a 30-inch Efgeeco triangular model, was too small - there was no way this giant would fold into the mesh.

Thinking quickly, Chris told me to get the keepnet out of the car; it was 6ft long and 18inches in diameter - he told me to attach a bankstick and we would try to bring the net up behind the fish to get it ashore. After a few attempts, success came our way, and both of us heaved the pike onto the bank.

Unhooking the fish with forceps - the hooks only just in the scissors - a set of Samson scales weighing up to 25lb were used to weigh her, but they bottomed out even before the fish's body had left the ground - what a dilemma. The fish lay in the keepnet still, and measured against the rings, spaced a foot apart, she was measured at four feet - 48 inches. She was carrying spawn; her girth was immense. We rested her in the keepnet in the margins while Chris debated what to do next. Was it really important to know the true weight, or was it enough to know he had caught one so big that he 'didn't need to lie'?

I can't remember why a member of the fishing club came along - walking his dog, I believe; he was shown the pike, and immediately went to his car to fetch a set of bigger scales - a pair

of 32lb Avons, but these suffered the same fate, bottoming out with some of the fish still touching the ground.

How big was she? Every winter for the next few years, the angling press would publish pictures and reports of big pike, with Neville Flicking, Dennis Pye, and other pike-fishing luminaries holding pike of 30lb+ to 40lb+ from the Norfolk Broads. Every time Chris saw them, he would look at me and say: "MINE WAS BIGGER THAN THAT, WASN'T IT?" Neither of us would disagree.

A few years later, Chris recalled a visit to the small lagoon joining the main one up in the North-East corner. Whilst playing a pike of about 6lb that he had hooked on a plug, a giant pike even bigger than the one he landed drifted up underneath and grabbed the smaller one across its jaws. This fish did come adrift after about five minutes, becoming bored with holding the other pike as Chris kept trying to pull them both up out of the snag-pit of sunken cars and concrete slabs. What the North Lagoon held has stayed a mystery to this day, and unless one has been caught by someone else who does not seek glory, we will never know.

CHAPTER FIVE

THE SEED GROWS INTO THE PLANT – KIDDIE-STEPS INTO THE ADULT WORLD

September 1969, a milestone: starting Secondary school, a brave new world from which the young mind started to branch out. Life felt so much bigger than the childish toys and games played before. No one told me that it would be so scary, though; not familiar with the rules, I fell victim to the bullying of the older and bigger boys, and even the smaller lads who had inveigled themselves into the gangs picked on me. Fights in the garages after school, arriving home with bloodied nose and ripped trousers, patching myself up before mum or Chris got home from work... Both were supportive; mum, however, still subscribed to the 'Big boys don't cry' mentality, which seemed difficult when you hurt so much.

It had all started badly for me, having started school three days after all the other first-year pupils. The family had returned from our first holiday with Chris, having spent two weeks travelling in the Lake District and up to Fort William on the west coast of Scotland. The holiday was a totally new experience; we had never been anywhere except day trips to Hastings, Southend, or Point Clear near Clacton in Essex. A fortnight seemed like a year, to explore and seek out new activities.

The first week, we stayed in a caravan on a farm near Lake Windermere, next to the cow field. Stepping down from the caravan, an eye had to be kept for fresh cow-pats, and all of us stood in at least one most days. We had never experienced anything like it; the smell was overpowering, and the mud so thick - I do not know how mum managed! It rained almost all week; there was enough dry weather, though, to allow us to go to Lake Coniston, where we skimmed stones, and to go boat-fishing on Lake Windermere, plug-fishing for pike with little hope of catching anything. On the Thursday, it rained so hard that Chris drove us to Blackpool, where we climbed the Tower and went swimming in the international-sized pool, where we witnessed someone belly-flop off the high board. He was a big man, and the splash seemed like an eruption; his stomach was bright red as he climbed from the water, and the lifeguard insisted he went to see a doctor. It wasn't all fun, though; having some time to kill, mum said we would go to the pictures, and the film that was playing was one none of us wanted to see - Tommy Steele in 'Half a Sixpence' - but we were only glad it wasn't 'The Sound of Music - mum would have sat there singing!

The week flew by, and before we knew it we were in Chris's little Hillman Imp, heading for Scotland. It was loaded down to the gunnels: three massive suitcases, food for another week of self-catering (tins of new potatoes, baked beans, corned beef, luncheon meat, etc.), and five people. How it ever survived is a mystery - driving through, up, and down mountain passes, it never broke down, and brought us safely home.

Fishing was attempted on this part of the holiday: free-lining bread-flake in the River Ness next to the caravan, parked in a small-holding – well, someone's back garden. Worm float-fished in Loch Ness - nothing was caught; expectancy was there, the fish were not.

The return journey was too far to make in one day, so a detour was made into the Lakes again. We felt like Joseph and Mary looking for somewhere to stay in the story of Jesus; there was no room at the inn. Nowhere being available for us to stay, Chris took us back to the farm, and they agreed to help. They had a small caravan parked near the top of the road leading up Cartmel Fell, one of the local peaks.

If we had thought the thirteen nights before had been an adventure, this raised the level to the max. The caravan was parked on a steep slope, at a forty-five-degree angle sideways, leaning against the stone wall beside the road. Sheep were grazing close by, and the wind was blowing a gale, rocking the caravan dangerously. We had no choice but to stay, and all of us children, even though excited, were filled with fear and anxiety.

Even the caravan held a surprise: it only had a double bed - two berths to fit five - almost an impossibility. Yet we did it; the three boys 'top and tailed' in the bed, while mum and Chris sat in the chairs all night, not getting any sleep. All night long the caravan rocked, and the wind whistled; we were all pleased and relieved when the sun broke over the horizon and we could make our escape back to Harlow New Town in Essex.

It is surprising how things can be forgotten. In the planning for the holiday, mum had not taken me shopping for my new school uniform. Monday came, and I had no long trousers, so I was sent to Senior school in the short ones worn in Primary school. How humiliating: I was pushed and teased, and even after Chris took me shopping to buy the required trousers at the weekend, the bullying continued. It was either grow strong or get used to it.

Sometime during that first year, I promised myself that the beatings, the laughter, the teasing would not hurt me. Instead of crying, I learnt to laugh in the bullies' faces; the punches stopped causing pain, and I would comment: "Is that the best you can do?" before walking away. Was it because they became bored, or because they realised that someone had stood up to them, that some even started to respect me, quietly becoming friends instead of enemies?

Fishing provided a common ground between us; they enjoyed going to the local river, where we found an interest that bridged the gap, and friendships started that would last throughout school. Six of us even started our own small fishing club, holding matches amongst ourselves for a small trophy at the end of the fishing season in March.

Mishaps would happen; youngsters would play - the need for watercraft and quiet movements was still a long way off. It was the being there that counted; the camaraderie was more important. One winter's trip to the River Stort for pike ended up with me having a gaff pushed through my right leg. Fortunately, the hook went straight through the muscle tissue, not drawing any blood, so we just continued fishing and mucking about. Nowadays, it would be home and then to A & E for a tetanus jab and stitches.

Not only was fishing fun, but the club also felt making our own tackle would be interesting, too. Our first attempts involved making floats with hard-paper bodies. The stem would be either a length of peacock quill or Indian reed, while the bodies would be made by cutting a piece of card into a long triangle. The long end was glued before rolling it onto itself, gluing the finished product. Amazingly, the floats performed well, and were still being used well into my teenage years. They could be made to suit still-water fishing, or, with the body high on the stem, they became great Avon floats for trotting the stream.

It was during my early life that the realisation came that I wasn't particularly good with my hands in craftwork, the making of fishing tackle highlighting the difficulty when we attempted to make pike plugs out of balsa-wood. Using a Stanley knife to shape the balsa, the top of my index finger of my right hand was sliced badly, and the scar can still be seen today.

CHAPTER SIX

THE PLANT BRANCHES OUT –

Parts of this chapter were included in another book, 'Barbel Tales', by a collection of writers brought together by the Barbel Society. It was published in its original form in 2013. The chapter was called 'Faded Memories'. The Society have kindly given me permission to publish it again here.

There were still a few more years of innocence left before the distractions of early teenage years crashed forcefully into my life. It would be three years before rock, the progressive rock sounds of Pink Floyd, Genesis and Yes, and the harder psychedelic sounds of Hawkwind, Tangerine Dream, et al, would take me to places in my mind to which, perhaps, in hindsight I should never have gone. Study took a back seat; parties and concerts beckoned, leading to a misspent youth, a life that now is remembered in a dream-like state, as though it was not my own.

The joy of going on holiday to somewhere new excited me; travelling down the old A30 to Christchurch in the old Hillman Imp, loaded to the gunnels, a fishing holiday beckoned. The family were on holiday; mother, stepfather and the three brothers, David, Jeff, and Paul (me) at Grove Farm Caravan Park on the banks of the Dorset Stour in Christchurch in the summer of 1970. Days were filled with fishing or going to the beach, either at Shell Bay or Boscombe, swimming and just having fun.

On the river, the preferred method of fishing was with a float set shallow for the plentiful dace, which would hang themselves on a size 18 hook and two maggots. Some days I would go to the weirpool at the bottom of the playing fields to touch-leger cheese-paste for the chub. I do remember my stepfather catching some wonderful-sized perch on worm in the run-off from the pool, where I watched mum fall into the water after placing her chair onto a cress-bed - oh how the sons laughed!

After several days, I became less interested in the beach, and after a mackerel-fishing trip out of Poole the day before, I just wanted to stay at the caravan to get over the queasiness left over from the seasickness. When the rest of the family wanted to go to the beach, I threw a paddy and dug my heels in. In those days, parents felt safer about their children than we do in our present society. With glee, I remember the feeling of sheer joy of being left alone to explore and do as I please. I promised not to stray from the caravan park, and watched them drive away in the trusty little Hillman Imp,

As soon as the car disappeared from sight, I excitedly walked down to the river, finding a peaceful spot in the uncut grass on the edge of the playing field to watch the clouds go by. Lying on my back without a care in the world, the innocence of childhood, the imagination seeing faces, animals, and mythical creatures in the shapes of clouds. After a while I remembered the river a few feet away, so, turning over onto my chest, I slowly edged myself forward till the reflection of my face was broken by the rippled, moving surface. Looking down into the shaded water under the tall bank, the two-foot drop to the water created shadow due to the height of the sun behind me; I could see a short, clear gravel run eight feet long and about three feet wide. The fronds of streamer and other weeds swayed in the current, and dace, small roach, gudgeon and minnows danced in the stream, looking for morsels of food.

Mesmerised, I hadn't noticed that a new shape had joined in the picture - how could a fish of such stature appear like a ghost? It had drifted out of the weed so slowly, and blended in with the surroundings so well... amazed, I was transfixed. Five feet below my face, it took up station; requiring little movement, it lay there for me to witness. Never having seen a barbel, my knowledge was based on pictures from the angling press and books that were now swimming in my mind. Fortunately, the fish helped with a flash of its side, giving me a clearer view of the mouth with its four barbules waving at the corners, reaching out to touch and taste the environment in which it lived. The long-ago memory of seeing that first barbel, a fish of monstrous proportions to the twelve-year old watching it from above, stayed with me, to light the fire of obsession many years later.

My heart skipped a beat, and the wish to jump up and let out a shout was held back; excitement fuelled by adrenaline made me light-headed - it was almost too much to bear. Lying in the current below was a fish I estimated at around thirty inches long. It held station for three or four minutes before drifting back under the weed from where it had come. I couldn't hold myself back any longer; I leaped up and laughed until I almost cried. The sick feeling felt earlier in the day was long forgotten, and I raced back to the caravan for my totally unsuitable tackle.

Walking back to the hallowed spot, there were no thoughts of how I would land this giant, no thoughts of even hooking it - just a need to be there with a slim chance to catch this monster that filled my soul with anticipation. I fished for over an hour, catching dace and roach, sending anything of worth - and the barbel - into hiding.

I didn't see the barbel again in that hole all week, and I returned home dreaming of catching one like it. That was all it became, though, as through the years the distraction of other fish took first place in my fishing, and it would not be until 2008 that I caught one anywhere near its size.

The following two seasons after that first glorious vision of beauty gave me opportunities of catching nice barbel. During the summer holidays from school, I would spend two or three days each week fishing. My friend Kevan and I would be dropped at Harlow train station by our parents for a journey down to Broxbourne on the banks of the River Lea. We weren't interested in the nearest stretch of river, though; our thoughts were on Kings Weir, a walk of over two miles downstream. The walk never seemed to get shorter, laden down with rod holdall and wicker baskets, plus enough food and bait to make us both walk lopsided and need to stop to change the tackle over to the other shoulder when it got too much. To get onto the lower London Anglers' Association stretch, the walk would entail walking along the long lock-cut before going over the bridge at the lock. Those last few hundred yards along the lock-cut seemed like an eternity; we were tired, but the thoughts of all the wonderful fish would keep us marching. Some days our limbs required a rest, so my stepfather would drop us off at Dobbs Weir in Hoddesdon, where it was a gentle two-hundred-yard walk to the swims in the weirpool.

In those heady summer days of youth, we were happy to catch anything that swam. Occasionally, the belief that we could catch the better fish would surface, yet as patience failed and quickly evaporated, we would return to the ever-present roach, dace and gudgeon. At Kings Weir, Kevan perfected a hemp-and-tare approach, and most days returned home with up to 50lb of chub and roach to boast about. My style of fishing relied on a light peacock waggler (unpainted and home-made) and small cubes of luncheon meat cast under the fronds of the willow trees, catching chub up to 31/2 lb for a similar total catch. Once in a while, a change of method would give exciting sport; floating crust would have the chub crashing into a frenzy, while swan-shot-link touch-legering with luncheon meat as bait produced constant action from the chub - and gave me my first barbel.

I can't remember much about my first barbel, but I do remember it couldn't have been bigger than 1lb. We would fish a deep eddy above the last riffle as the water left the LAA stretch; bites came thick and fast, and on good days forty or fifty barbel and chub would tug the line out of my fingers. The beauty of these small barbel will also stay with me - perfection in miniature, gleaming with health, some as small as large gudgeon, the length of my hand, fitting in my palm; care was taken not to harm something so glorious.

From the school holiday summers, another memory stands out, losing my first large(?) barbel. Memories distort, and in the mind of a young teenager size does expand. This fish wasn't under my eyes only five feet away; it lay on the edge of the willow fronds against the opposite bank, some thirty–five feet away. Casting a light waggler rig baited with a small cube of luncheon meat on a size 12 hook, aided by a new Bruce and Walker CTM 14a rod and 2lb Bayer Perlon line, the rig landed inches off the trailing fronds. Straightening the line, the float moved a few feet before darting swiftly away. I struck, not prepared for the consequences; the rod buckled, and amazingly the fish bored into a small weed-bed and stopped. In the shallow thirty inches of clear water, I could see the flashing of a barbel of similar proportions to the one seen three years before at Christchurch.

Without hesitation, I started to enter the shallow water to wade across and hopefully free the fish, and to have a chance of landing it. But my worst nightmare appeared! The bailiff, a real kill-joy and jobsworth, appeared behind me to check my ticket. Now I wasn't worried by that, as an LAA licence sat at the bottom of my tackle box; no, I knew he would tell me that wading was not allowed and to come back to the bank. My pleas of a monster barbel and not wanting to lose it fell on deaf ears, and as I turned to wade back to the bank, the rod in my hands pulled down flat as the barbel swam away, and the line fluttered in the breeze, coming back without a hook.

Anger boiled within me, but knowing it wouldn't bring the fish back, I splashed ashore, kicking the water towards the bailiff. He responded in his normal manner, giving me a ticking-off about breaking the rules, and telling me that if he caught me again, I would be banned. However firm he was, we knew that he would forget this misdemeanour - as he had before!

Other such encounters may have taken place in those summer days. At Dobbs Weir, unstoppable fish would be hooked on swimfeedered maggot or legered luncheon meat fished off the weir wall, casting into the white water below. Were they barbel? It was difficult to tell, for the pool held large carp; is it important now? Memories of lost fish are hopefully lessons learned, if nothing else than to use more suitable, balanced tackle in the future.

CHAPTER SEVEN

THE PLANT WITHERS –
A YEAR IN THE WILDERNESS

During my last year at school, between the ages of fifteen and sixteen, fishing was still on the radar. However, the pull of a life full of risk and fun drew me away into a nether-world, filled with demons. Having hidden the pain of childhood, parents divorcing, being bullied, and feeling unloved, it became a self-fulfilling prophesy, convincing myself that I was not loved, and that no one else would love me, either.

At the time, though, it felt full of excitement, attending rock concerts, and going to crazy parties; travelling by train with a friend to be at the Charlton football ground to see The Who, Humble Pie, Lou Reed, Lindisfarne, Montrose, Bad Company and Maggie Bell; all for £2.50! A great day, spoilt by the worst sunburn I have had - and seeing Pink Floyd at the Rainbow in November 1973, at their benefit for Robert Wyatt of Soft Machine.

Many other groups were seen over a period of about eighteen months. Harlow New Town, my home, put on free concerts every fortnight of the summer at our own miniature Crystal Palace Bowl - a small stage with a shallow pool in front, with space filled with a crowd of over twenty thousand fans watching. Between 1972 and 1974, these concerts were packed out, hosting acts as famous as 10cc, The Groundhogs, Renaissance, Steeleye Span, Pink Fairies and Arthur Brown. The council made one mistake, though: getting the Bay City Rollers to appear. That day, over forty thousand children and parents wrecked the park area, which nearly brought a close to the concerts altogether.

Every year, Hawkwind would play the last night, and in both 1972 and '73, we were treated to the full 'Space Ritual' set, with Stacia dancing and Michael Moorcock narrating. No trouble ever beset these nights; there may have been drugs and underage drinking taking place, yet the police kept a low profile, and the evenings always passed peacefully.

1974 saw a different set from Hawkwind. I had returned from the family's new home in the Fens of Cambridgeshire, where we had moved three months before. The album 'Hall of the Mountain Grill' had been released a month or so before, prompting the band to play the album without any other tunes. The audience became irate and called out for more; of course, the band obliged and started to ask for what we wanted to hear. Fortunately, I was standing feet away from the stage, on the narrow wall between the pool and stage. Everyone appeared to be shouting out for 'Silver Machine', the band's hit single; however, as the calls died down and the band took stock, I called out for another song: 'Orgone Accumulator'. To my surprise,

Dave Brock looked in my direction, nodded, and said something to the band - the song played was mine!

Even though fishing appeared to have taken a back seat, visits to the River Lea at Dobbs Weir still took place, more often than not fishing the lock-cut, catching small roach and dace. When driving across the road bridge at the tail of the weirpool, it was not possible to see the water below; however, walking it enabled you to see a short piece of bank downstream of the bridge - we called it the free stretch. All the other water available to fish was controlled by the LAA, except a short piece owned by a private landowner, who ran the swims on the road bank of the pool.

The free stretch was secluded; no one ever came down to look, and we felt it was just our own. The mystery of the fishing was discovered, as a few years before boredom had set in with trying to catch something more than gudgeon and bleak, both being numerous in those days; a walk with a rod and some dead bleak saw me standing looking over the bridge, away from the weir. With nothing better to do, a bleak was impaled onto a size 8 hook and lowered down the twenty feet to the water. No thought was given to landing a fish - I didn't even have a landing net with me.

The breeze picked up the line, and the bleak hung on the surface; as I let some more line off the reel, it started to drift downstream. Before it had travelled more than thirty feet, a dark shadow rose behind it; a large white mouth opened, and the bleak disappeared as the chub - for that is what it was - sank from view. Striking into thin air, I wondered what had happened; the line had been bitten through by the chub's throat teeth.

For the next few years, we would try to tempt these chub, for it was a shoal that resided there, and somewhere in the region of a dozen of these leviathans could be seen in the best conditions - but we never did catch one. The nearest I came to catching was from the bank down on the free stretch on a trip during the latter years explored in this chapter.

After much thought, I came up with a method using a short, thick length of unpainted peacock quill, my favourite floats, attached bottom only and locked in place by two AAA shot, with the hook baited with a dead bleak or gudgeon, two feet below. In the right conditions, a strong breeze blowing upstream, with the rod held high, gave the best chance of fooling the chub into making a mistake.

Catching a few bleak for bait, I readied myself for the hope of a giant swimming into the bottom of the landing net. The breeze was exactly right; the cast, though difficult through the overhanging branches, landed where I wanted, and with the rod held high enough in between them a bait was drifted downstream in the middle of the river. Most casts did see the float shooting under, but very few made contact; no bite-offs occurred, though. I had little idea how the chub took the bait; my understanding now is they would swallow the bait to their throat teeth, with their mouth open wide - therefore, all I succeeded in doing was pulling the hook straight back out again.

Perseverance paid off in the end, but the two fish landed were minnows compared to the fish seen most days. Both were only 2lb 8oz; another larger fish was hooked, but the hooked pulled as it battled close to the rod-tip. This was the last time I ever fished there, as the family moved to Guyhirn, near Wisbech in Cambridgeshire; it would be several years till the next time a chub would see the end of my line.

CHAPTER EIGHT

A RURAL BEGINNING.

Can the city be taken out of the boy; can the boy be taken out of the city? When we moved from Bow in London to Harlow New Town, even if the environment saw a defined change, it was nothing as compared to the continental shift of moving to the Fens of Cambridgeshire. However, in hindsight, it was the best thing that could have happened - even though, for a decade, life continued in disarray, falling into the same traps, straying to rock concerts, parties, drugs and drink, lessons were always there to be learnt, yet mistakes won more often than not until the age of twenty-five.

....

The move to Cambridgeshire in 1974 was a real culture-shock. Not only did the life of the village and surrounding area seem dull, but if a child had not done geography at school, they would never know what a hill was! The land, all below sea level, protected by the levee running along the tidal River Nene, which flowed on the opposite side of the road to our house, was flat as a pancake; farm fields unbroken by hedges, an occasional lonely tree - nothing obscured the view for miles, except of course the levee.

Having left school on the day of moving, I travelled from Harlow by train, after finishing Biology, the last of three O- level examinations; Chris, mum, and Jeff, my youngest brother, had left two days before with the removal lorry, leaving me with family friends, who made sure no trouble befell me, basically having me on lock-down, not allowed out after school. I understood the reason, as only a few weeks before I had been in hospital, when an ill-thought overdose resulted in a two-day hospital stay.

The move took place in June; we arrived to bright, sunny days, gentle breezes blew across the Fens during daylight hours, lulling us into a false sense of security, for when the winds blew they really did blow over the flat, empty landscape. It had been agreed that work was not the most important choice I should make; an agreement was made with mum and Chris that I would attend college in September to retake examinations failed earlier in the year.

This gave me an opportunity to explore the local rivers and drains, the land drainage canals throughout the Fens to keep the water table at the right levels to ensure the Fens did not flood. Even though the tidal Nene was only twenty-five yards from our front door, it was the Twenty Foot Drain two miles away that took first cast. As with most of the drains, the Twenty Foot had been cut in a straight line across the landscape; the depths ranged from three feet down to twelve, appearing to be equal three-foot steps in depth. Along both bank-side margins grew vast lily-beds; the only gaps had been cut by the local angling club to facilitate the matches fished there.

In every drain, the fish stock consisted of bream, pike, zander, roach and tench. During the winter months, specimen hunters would descend and leapfrog their way along the drain, fishing up to four rods, even before it was legal, and reports of pike to over 30lb were seen in the angling press most weeks until March 14th.

Chris, who had been an avid pike angler before the move, did not fish much, and it was not obvious why! He stopped fishing until a decade later, when his interest was rekindled by our joining a small syndicate lake, with a nice head of stunning carp.

What took my interest were the tench, fishing for them with the Avon rod I had built several years before, tackling up with the lift method, and dropping the bread bait into holes in the lily-beds on the shallow inside ledge. The tackle stood the test; with 6lb line, very few fish did not make it to the bank. None were of specimen size, with the best a fraction under 5lb; however, it was great fun.

On one occasion, something truly unstoppable was hooked, and my belief it was a carp was not disproved; I would go on to land a few from another drain even closer to home.

As a distraction, one weekend I foolishly entered a match fished on the Twenty Foot Drain. The matches always attracted top match anglers from further afield, and this weekend was no exception; I was overwhelmed, being drawn next to Kevin Ashurst on one side and Ivan Marks the other! What is worse, we were pegged on top of one of the resident bream shoals - hundreds of fish packed into about forty yards of drain, covering four pegs. The shoal hugged the far-bank drop-off, requiring leger tackle fished over groundbait. The bream were hungry, but unfortunately my standard of fishing fell far short of the two 'Superstars', who bagged over 50lb each, while I managed one bream for 2lb 8oz...

Over the years, I had been bought several nice items of fishing tackle as presents, and one had until now gathered dust. I had asked Chris and mum for a centrepin reel two years before, but the distractions of rock music and parties meant it had been left in its box. The reel was a Grice and Young Gypsy Coq d'Or, a real workhorse that still serves me now. Daylight beckoned it when I started to fish the tidal river across from the house, and in the outlet for Morton's Leam quarter of a mile upstream.

Trotting was only really possible on the higher tides; the depth of sediment was dangerous, and not even a fool would risk walking out on it. The tidal drop was over twelve feet, which exposed the mud out to a distance of twenty feet or more. The method used to catch fish was simple: laying-on in the small bays created in the bank by the current, and roach and bream up to 2lb in weight would come regularly to the net. Almost every day, large unstoppable fish were hooked; again, the culprits were carp. In the outlet, this happened even more often, sometimes a couple of times a day, but if we stepped up the strength of tackle the bites would slow. My friends and I wanted to catch fish, so we plugged away, accepting these losses as the price.

The carp obsession had not bitten yet; however, this soon changed at the beginning of the 1979 season. Returning home after working a summer season at Butlin's, rest was on the agenda. The camp I worked at was in Skegness, Lincolnshire; I only survived till July, being sent home with a box of strong antibiotics! The stories of chalet parties with smuggled-in drink from the nearest off-licence fuelling the close physical bonding are all true. The reality involved 24/7 work and parties; little sleep was had by the staff, and it was surprising anyone lasted a complete season.

A week later found me enjoying a warm evening on the banks of Morton's Leam, fishing above the sluice-gate, laying-on with bread-flake in the hope of a tench or two. Nothing had been caught except a few greedy roach which engulfed a size 8 hook, so when the float lifted and lay flat, an expected tench turned into a carp as its first run went under the railway bridge twenty yards to my left and carried on going! Six-pound line and an Avon rod seemed to be insignificant, yet the fish stopped, coming back towards me, thankfully keeping out of the lily-beds lining both sides of the drain. As the fish came level, I hoped it would stop, but it still kept going, only being stopped in its path by the sluice-gate thirty yards to my right.

For forty minutes, the carp just plodded up and down, and I am unsure why it gave up and swam into the net; it had plenty of strength left to break free, as it thrashed in the over-small landing net. At 26lb 5oz, my largest fish by a fair margin, the next best being an honest 9lb 15oz pike, I was over the moon. The capture had been witnessed by a few other lads, one having a camera with them.

It was a few more years till I would be able to travel for my fishing, on a 100cc motor bike, sounding more like a bee in a tin can; that carp really took over, and for a period of thirty years, they became my life, the true obsession.

CHAPTER NINE

FREEDOM TO GROW – STILL SCARED OF THE DARK!

The freedom a young man achieves when released from the distance he can walk or has to rely on dad or mum's taxi - a world of wonder, to explore without the confines of the family.

By 1975, a place at Isle of Ely College, re-sitting all the examinations taken at school - even the better subjects like biology had been a failure - took up time; I would have liked to be out fishing. More hours were given to a part-time job in the local supermarket (Key Markets, a supermarket chain no longer with us, had just opened the first supermarkets of over 25,000 square feet, one of them being in Wisbech, the large town nearby), collecting the trolleys and sweeping the shop floor before closing time four evenings a week. In those days, shops didn't open all night or even on a Sunday.

One evening sticks in my mind: June 4th, 1975. After a sunny day, from nowhere, a snowstorm hit East Anglia; over two inches fell, making collecting the 400 trolleys from the car park fun. The day was immortalised by a track on the album 'Trick of the Tail' recorded later that year by the band Genesis, called 'Mad Man Moon'. The line in the song went '... and the evil of a snowflake in June could still be a sign of relief'; the song may not have been written because of that storm - however, it gave me a reference point in my memory.

Mum and Chris had agreed that if I studied hard and worked to fund some of my spending, they would buy me a motorbike; well, that was a bit of a misnomer, as it was a 100cc Suzuki, with a top speed of 50mph - with a good tail-wind... The opportunities to travel with fishing tackle had not really been thought about, and trying to carry a rod holdall and a basket on the back of the seat became a balancing act, needing a lot of practice.

Night of the Rats - Fear of the dark!

One of the first fisheries more distant than the local drains I visited was a group of lakes near Downham Market, fifteen miles away. These day-ticket waters, I now believe, were called Woodlakes; apart from the main lake, they had been left undisturbed, and were a perfect place to try night-fishing for the first time. In 2021, the complex was a holiday site, with caravans dotted throughout; however, they still can be fished on a day-ticket, as they were then.

The lakes that took my fancy were the smaller two, neither bigger that a couple of acres. These were likely to have been the original lakes on site; both had undulating bottoms, were full of weed, and both only had depths up to five feet maximum. In the summer of 1976, the drought was imprinted on the memory of anyone alive at the time, and the area of water shrank to less than half. Daytime fishing became impossible, so a few friends and I decided we would night-fish. Another of my local favourite waters, the Twenty Foot Drain, only had water in the deepest central channel, meaning it had dropped nine feet, and was carrying a sixtieth of the total volume of water it should be.

There are some fears we do not share with our friends, as we know boys are not afraid of anything, RIGHT...? If all of us could be honest, we would have admitted to some fears that would have us laughing at ourselves now. As a young boy, I would suffer nightmares and hide away from scary television shows like 'Dr Who'...Ha-ha! - and believe ghosts would come to haunt me. Even into my teenage years, the fears might have changed, but there were still things that frightened me. One of them was rats, thankfully now a long-gone faded memory.

So, the chosen night to spend at the lakes arrived, and three of us set up on the larger of the two small lakes. The beach I sat upon had surfaced that summer on the bar between two islands, which seemed a great place to fish. The amount of tackle that could be carried on the motorbike didn't allow for a sun-bed; we didn't have proper fishing bedchairs in those days! A small Lafuma low-chair would be the place to rest my head; however, as the night progressed, sleep came upon me.

Not having anywhere to lay my head, I foolishly decided to use the large uncut loaf I had taken for bait as a pillow. Lying on the ground and folding my knees into my chest helped me to keep warm; the summer heat had fallen sharply under a cloudless sky; sleep came slowly, unable to keep my eyes open, overly tired, and exhausted. However, a sudden noise by my ear startled me. My turning over most likely scared whatever had made the noise; nothing was there, so I tried to sleep once more.

The disturbance happened several times; I became worried - keeping my eyes open, I was determined to find out what had caused the noise. Several minutes passed before a horrible apparition appeared before my eyes - a large brown rat approached my face, only inches away, wanting to eat into the loaf. I jumped out of my skin – well, not quite - but in my haste to scare it off, I rolled straight into the water. Both my friends came noisily round to see what the commotion was. Their first reaction was to laugh loudly at me, standing in the lake margin, soaked from rolling into the water. However, after telling them of the rats, they became a bit edgy, too. It was a long night; even though it was late June, when sunrise was around 4.00am, the daylight couldn't come quickly enough.

It would be several years before an attempt to night-fish again was made. Fortunately, the fear of what goes bump in the night has long gone; I enjoy spending a few hours into dark if the conditions are favourable, yet it isn't something I do often. The need to night-fish, in my opinion, does not enable the angler to catch more fish, unless that is the only time they may have available. Personally, the opportunity to see everything that goes on, to be able to sight-hunt fish in shallow water, to catch when many 'specimen hunters' will not be fishing, is the challenge.

Achieving your captures, doing it your own way, in your own time, using watercraft you have learnt over the years, is something I think is more important than catching the best or most.

Of Carp, close encounters, and accidents

It wasn't just Woodlakes that was visited; another couple of different venues, North-West of Guyhirn, came to my notice. One was the upper River Welland, and the other was a gravel pit near Deeping St James. Both were controlled by the Deeping St James angling club; however, the ride on the bike was further, over twenty miles, but it was worth it.

Chub were the target on the river, having not caught any since 1973 at Dobbs Weir on the River Lea. The methods used were simple: either trotting a small waggler float in water no deeper than three feet with maggot as bait, catching several in a swim before moving to another swim downstream, or rolling luncheon meat and using floating crust. There were a couple of giant chub in the small weirpool in the town of Deeping St James itself; everything was tried to trick them, but to no avail.

Here, I learnt that fear can be overcome. A remarkably close encounter of the reptile kind was an epiphany moment worth sharing. The afternoon was very hot and sticky; the fishing was difficult, stalking the chub in the pool run-off, crawling through the grass and weeds growing almost three feet tall. The chub I was after could be seen lying against the bank a little further downstream; slowly, I approached with all the stealth of a big cat, hoping not to disturb it. Suddenly a rustling noise came to my attention close by in the long grass - without warning, the head of a snake, with a big red 'V' marking, appeared inches from my nose!

There was no time for fear; I quietly and smoothly moved my body backwards until I was able to rise up onto my lower legs. The adder hissed and moved its head side to side, but it came no nearer, nor tried to move away. Slowly, I raised myself up to my full height, and as I did so, the snake moved towards my legs, gilding over my wader-covered feet, turning its head to hiss at me one last time before sliding off into the grass, not to be seen again.

The lakes held different challenges: gin-clear water, old gravel workings with plenty of gravel bars and weed, and carp to be caught. My true carp fishing days hadn't started yet; perhaps this was my apprenticeship. My tackle consisted of the old Avon rod I had made for myself, 6lb line, and a free-lined piece of bread-flake. I had read articles and heard tales in hushed tones about the baits now being used for carp, but the new style of fishing was beyond my financial abilities.

The carp living in the pit grew to low twenties, so my tackle could be seen as totally under-gunned; yet, in my innocence, it had to be tried – 'In for a penny, in for a pound' came to mind. My first Sunday visit found a pit empty of anglers, giving plenty of choice of swims to fish. Choosing a point swim, I was given a vast area of water to fish, but using free-lined bread-flake I could fish no more than thirty feet from the bank. The rod was set on a couple of low rests, the tip pointing at the water's surface. After sinking the line, it was allowed to hang slack, and a washing-up bottle-top was used as a bite indicator - not that I would need one, though!

As I sat watching the water, several carp could be seen drifting just under the surface, not far from where I had cast. Lulled by the sun and warm breeze, I was hypnotised by the ripples of the water's surface. Suddenly, the rod dived forward; fortunately, sitting right next to the rod- butt, I was able to grab it before it disappeared to be towed across to the other side of the pit. This happened twice during the afternoon. Both fish were weighed as low doubles, the larger was 14lb 9oz, followed by 11lb 12oz - the first time in a day two carp were caught.

On occasion, I wouldn't take the fishing tackle out with me, but just go for a ride to seek out other fishing venues to try. One such journey a year later could have been my last - it was for the bike! Having been out all day, the journey home took me past the banks of the lower River Welland outside Spalding In Lincolnshire. The back-wind propelled me and the bike at a speed of over 50mph; a surprise, something that did not happen

often. With a pair of Optix sunglasses on under the visor, and just a tee-shirt, I imagined being Jack Nicholson in 'Easy Rider', a cult movie of the late 1960s.

The road had recently been covered in a new layer of tarmac and gravel chippings. I came to a sharp left-hand bend; leaning over low to keep up my speed, I was unaware of a pile of gravel chippings had been left unswept at the apex of the corner. The next thing I knew, the bike was on its side, sliding towards a barbed-wire fence put there to protect the cattle grazing on the grass by the river. In slow motion, my crash-helmet came adrift, and my sunglasses shattered in front of my eyes as I rolled off the bike just before it smashed into a concrete fence-post.

Amazingly, I walked away: the glass from the sunglasses did not enter my eyes, and my only injuries were a grazed knee and torn trousers. However, the bike was a different story completely: the front forks, which took the full force of the impact against the post, were bent at an angle, impossible to ride.

It wasn't until many months later that I passed my driving test and bought my first car. I never had the same enthusiasm to ride a bike again.

CHAPTER TEN

MILTON FERRY AND CASTOR BACKWATER

It took three attempts to pass my driving test. Taking two of them at the age of seventeen, I had been incapable of achieving a pass; immaturity, chasing dreams and searching for myself in my navel took their toll. However, in June 1981, the stars aligned, and success was achieved while in a dream of a sleepless weekend.

At the time, my job was working in Fruit and Vegetable distribution, working a nightshift, six nights a week; it wasn't necessarily hard work - we were allowed to finish when the last order had been completed. At the beginning of the week, we would be home by 1.00am, but due to a lifestyle that included parties and late-night drinking, there was little hope of sleep. Pubs stayed open far too frequently in the Fens, not closing until the early hours of the morning.

Instead of fishing, the weekend of 17-19th June 1981 had been filled with attending a party in Cambridge on Saturday night. Travelling with some friends on Saturday morning, we made a day of it, before partying the night away. Somehow, I didn't manage any sleep on Sunday, either, before going to work. The shift was finished by 4.00am, but I didn't want to sleep and miss the driving test set for 9.00am on Monday.

I may have dozed, but at 9.00am sharp I arrived at the test centre; however, the examiner was my worst nightmare, Mr Flood, who had a reputation of not passing anyone, and as he had failed me before, I didn't hold much hope. I messed up the reading of the number plate, stalled the car leaving the centre, and even had to do a second emergency stop after a dog ran out in front of me. The lack of sleep must have relaxed me, however; there was no anxiety or rushing, and each mistake was followed by the correct response. After stalling, the handbrake was put on, engine switched off and taken out of gear; I turned the ignition key, looking for hazards before indicating and waiting to pull out.

All I can say is Mr Flood must have had a great weekend, for he gave me a pass, but I nearly threw it away when I said I would kiss him! He quickly rebutted this, saying that if I did that, he would fail me! Tiredness does funny things to the brain, making us do or say silly things, and that was ingrained on my memory for life.

Within days, a car had been purchased, a 1971 Ford Escort estate. The opportunity to travel bit hard; within two days, accompanied by a friend, it took me to North Wales, where we made Caernarfon car park our home for the week. The atmosphere was exciting, it being the eve of the royal wedding of Prince Charles and Lady Diana. A large screen of 26,000 light bulbs had been erected to show the event, and the lighting of the beacons across England and Wales to celebrate. All week long the crowds grew in number, coming from all over the world. During the daytime, we would travel elsewhere to get away from the whole business.

On the return journey, a mistake occurred that lessons from my past should have prevented; for the first and last time, thankfully. Leaving Caernarfon late at night meant driving until daylight next day; sometime about 4.00am, tiredness came upon me, and before I knew what had happened the car was bouncing off the kerb and swerving dangerously across the road. Fortunately, there were no other cars on the road - someone was watching over us. Bringing the car to a sudden halt and regaining my senses, I drove slowly to a lay-by a few hundred yards further down the road, where we rested for a couple of hours before continuing the journey, arriving back in Wisbech at 11.00am.

Later that summer, fishing came over my horizon again, and I was put back on the path by exploring the River Nene, near Peterborough. First stop was Castor Backwater, off the A47 on the way to Wansford. Away from the main river, this narrow little weed-clogged stream beckoned the fisherman inside to cast a line. The fast runs between bulrushes, the weirpool, the deep undercuts shaded by bushes, the big bay where the pike came to spawn at the end of each season - all encouraging a different approach to catch fish.

The Avon rod came out to play, loaded with 6lb Maxima, my line of choice during the 1970s, fishing either free-lined or with a quarter-ounce bomb. Baits for the chub included cheese, bread-crust, and luncheon meat, and for the roach and dace, mainly maggot or hemp. In 1981, barbel were not seen as a fish caught, and only one had ever been reported, a 12lb fish in 1969.

On many occasions, a cheese or luncheon-meat bait fished against the undercut was taken by an unseen leviathan; it would bend the light rod double, powering back into the undercut before the line would snap. Now I would use heavier line; however, I didn't carry any over 6lb in my tackle bag then.

Hooked and lost fish encouraged the purchase of a new rod. Not having many decent tackle shops in my local area that didn't major in match-fishing on the Fenland drains meant a journey to the Midlands, namely Birmingham, to the wonderful tackle emporium owned by Terry Eustace - a great angler, who greeted every angler as an equal in the shop. He would be willing to give advice, and the cup of tea or coffee served to all and sundry meant a trip to the shop would be a whole-day affair.

Terry helped me choose a rod that he felt would be suitable for my needs. I will always remember his way of selling this choice to me. He trusted everyone, so he gave me a made-up version of the rod and a reel loaded with line, telling me to go outside, put the line through the rod-rings, and tie it to the bars in front of the shop windows - for security, as it was a rough area of Birmingham! He encouraged you to flex the rod as hard as you could - much better than the shop-keeper grabbing the tip-eye and telling you to pull, which does not give a true action to the rod at all.

The rod I walked away with wasn't made up; I purchased a Spec Nine blank with a cork handle, plus the required eyes and whipping thread. Terry gave me the measurements for spacing the eyes to achieve the desired action. The joy of making my first rod for a few years returned, and the first fish, a 2lb chub, sealed the thrill.

If not using the Spec Nine, some days would be spent trotting for the chub with maggots at the end of the rapids, which would produce great sport. Using my CTM 14a rod and a 5x4 Pete Warren stick-float, a size 16 hook and double maggot was trotted over a handful of maggots every cast, and brought chub to the net regularly. The best I caught at the time was 4lb 9oz; there may have been larger, but what was more important - just catching or chasing the biggest?

The last two weeks of the fishing season saw an invasion of the Backwater, as pike in great numbers would arrive from the main river to spawn. The big females kept themselves back till after the 14th; only the hungry males kept the fisherman happy. The place to fish was a large bay on the top of the double bend, where now the flow has changed drastically, and the bay has shrunk at what is called the 'Gate Swim'. Currents would eddy slowly under the two willow trees, and a cast with a gudgeon caught earlier hooked on a size 2 single hook, suspended under a two swan-shot Peter Drennan loafer float, would quickly get a response.

My younger brother Jeff and I would spend a couple of hours catching the livebait - as well as chub and dace, which we returned - before moving to the eddy, taking it in turns to run a float around. On our best day, eighteen pike were netted; they were so hungry that, if the bait was dropped, you just left it where it was to be taken again. None weighed over 10lb, the best being 9lb 15oz, yet they kept you warm on a cold day.

Further downstream, the River Nene flowed under Milton Ferry bridge, long disused as a crossing except by foot, where the currents created a hotspot to catch chub. Casting from the cattle-drink on the northern bank into the middle arch and hitting the wall of the arch support, a bite would come as a boat passed. The habit of waiting for a boat to come along worked a treat; casting as it passed under the bridge, the rod-tip would indicate a take before I could put the rod in the rest. Using a quiver-tip screwed into the top eye of the Spec Nine, the bites would be delicate drop-backs, which without the quiver-tip would likely go unnoticed.

The River Nene held, and still holds, a reasonable head of carp, and the Milton Ferry section was no exception; in the right conditions, they would head-and-shoulder in the deep margin of the far bank. Only occasionally did I hook something that would suggest a carp, though; fishing the far bank, casting against the first bridge arch using cheese as bait, the bite, unlike anything else seen here, had me grasping for a rod diving into the water. The reel, a Mitchell 301, was back-winding, and I had difficulty grabbing the handle. Reaching the far bank, the fish turned and went upstream; still, as I was still using inadequate strength line it was goodbye fish.

It would be several years before I learnt the lesson, and scaled my tackle up to accommodate the species being fished for. However, success did come in other ways - the day trotting single bronze maggot under a 5x4 stick float close into the reeds below the rapids, producing a bag of chub up to 4lb 9oz; days floating crust further upstream by the bulrushes, again having chub after chub, which fought over the crust as it drifted downstream.

Success is measured in our own mind; the possibility of achieving someone else's is but a pipe-dream. My dreams are mine and yours belong to you; a man needs to be confident in his own success and only compete with himself. It is fighting that starts wars - two men seek the same goal and there will be a war; paraphrasing the philosopher Thomas Hobbes, who stated this in 1651, in his work on 'The Natural Condition of Mankind': "... if two men desire the same thing, which nevertheless they cannot enjoy, they become enemies...".

The obsession to catch the biggest, or most, had still not taken hold in my fishing; it was an unknown concept - fishing was fun, and an escape from the anxieties and fears that growing up presented. There is enough of a challenge to angling without competing against the self-esteem (or lack of) of others seeking the same goal.

CHAPTER ELEVEN

THE FENLAND MERES

My younger brother, Jeff, joined the Cambridge Police Force as a Cadet at seventeen; it was a profession he relished and enjoyed, staying within their ranks all his working life. This is now looked back on as a time when the ethics and behaviour of some officers were seen not to be politically correct, and if you asked, some of the force would agree. However, the social and political atmosphere of Britain was far removed from our present day, and the police have gone a long way to improving the general public's impression of them. A sign of those times was the joke by Birmingham comedian Jasper Carrott: "A good policeman takes his work home with him - he beats someone up in his living room".

Some types of employment enjoy the privilege of sports and social clubs; the police were no different, and one club in particular interested Jeff more than most - an active angling section that controlled some gravel pits in the flat Fens near to home, giving an opportunity to participate in some good fishing. The three pits, Honey Pond, Browns and Wimblington Mere, all had their own personalities. Honey, the oldest of the three, a small pit of less than an acre, was a maze of bays and islands, reed- fringed and shallow; hidden from the other two, a further hundred yards down the rutted track, few anglers bothered with it, yet for those that did, the rudd it held were worth the effort.

Browns was more of a square pit of about four acres, almost uniform in depth, with only a few lily-beds and one stretch of reeds, which made it less interesting to the majority of anglers, but in one corner a point jutted out, almost making a small pond

separate from the main body of water. This was where the pads grew, and a swim on the point gave access to a great spot to catch the small carp and tench the pit held.

The Mere was another completely different kettle of fish. A much larger area of water, covering about twelve acres of wind-swept water, it was more exposed to the elements; even with a high bank on one bank protecting the angler fishing at the bottom, the wind still blew in all directions, whipping up the surface except on the quietest days. A good head of crucian carp lived here, and many an hour was spent amassing good catches of them to a weight of just over 1lb.

Jeff belonged to the match-fishing section of the police club, who held regular matches on the Mere. Most competitions were won with over 20lb of crucians and small tench. On the first visits

I made here, as a guest of Jeff, we would spend the day fishing for these little bars of gold. The fishing was easy, as their patrol route took in the margins, and a flurry of five or six fish would be caught, followed by a lull until the fish returned ten minutes later. There were so many crucians in the Mere; there were shoals of them everywhere, waiting for a bait of sweetcorn or caster, their favourites, to be dropped in front of them.

After a few years, though, the Cambridge Police lost the pits to RMC, or as they became known, Leisure Sport. The season permit only cost £12, and covered a vast portfolio of lakes, pits, and rivers; inflation of unthinkable levels has since made those of us old enough wonder where those days have gone...!

We continued to fish the pits for another few years, mainly casting a line on Browns. Fun could be had float-fishing 8mm Richworth shelf-life boilies, bought in tiny pots and flavoured and soaked by ourselves to soften them, making them hookable on a size 10 hook, or a tiny cube of luncheon meat under a small peacock quill loaded by a swan-shot, two inches from the hook – the lift method at its best.

The carp on Browns were nearly all thin, almost wildie-like (the true variety brought into Britain by medieval monks for food) in appearance. There were only a handful of mirrors, including a beautiful perfectly-formed fully-scaled that never reached a weight of over 6lb in our time there. The heaviest Browns held was a leather with no scales upon its body, which at its top weight in 1987 went 15lb 10oz.

A return to the main Mere, fishing matching rods the following season, produced several carp caught on flavoured chickpeas. Casting to a point covered in an impervious jungle of bushes gave me a catch of two carp up to 18lb 12oz.

Another reason to be thankful to my brother Jeff: he found the syndicate lake, an impossible place to find in the middle of the vast, flat landscape of the Fens. It could be compared to an oasis in the desert; the trees surrounding the lake gave the

impression of a watering hole in a parched, empty landscape. Apart from the crops being grown in the fields, nothing broke the line of sight; the nearest farm buildings appeared as dots on the horizon, and the single-track path leading to it could not be seen from the nearest road - the perfect hideaway, which only fifteen of us had permission to fish.

I wasn't able to join the first year, as Jeff had invited our stepfather, Chris. He hadn't fished for many years since moving to Guyhirn in 1974; his health had taken a turn for the worse, and he had been diagnosed with emphysema, or what is now called COPD, a disease of the lungs that restricted the distance he could walk. Being able to drive right up to the lake, he was able to manage the complete circuit of the two-acre lake for several years before he would have to fish the car-park swim; here a bench was erected, and the swim was appropriately called Chris's Swim.

The carp weren't huge, but the challenge of catching them was, though. Joining Jeff and Chris the second season, I caught on the rare occasions when I visited the lake. Living in Watford and having the Colne Valley on my doorstep did not give me much encouragement to travel, but, when I did, the journey from door to lake could be done in one hour and a bit - if done in the early hours of the morning!

Distractions began to lead me away from fishing; the enjoyment sank, and only the occasional highlight would cheer me enough to carry on. However, as the obsession of carp fishing started to take hold, little else mattered.

Book TWO

The carp years

Obsession Personified

Till now, fishing had been fun, not taking up too much of my time; however, the Obsession silently entered by the back door, distracting me from the life path set before me.

CHAPTER TWELVE

DIPPING MY TOES - TOLPITS AND RICKMANSWORTH AQUADROME

August 1986: after spending six months in Northampton, running a small hostel housing homeless teenagers for a Christian charity, and living-in 24/7, I made a decision to apply for a position with Social Services, and my first application was successful. Requiring a move to Watford, Hertfordshire, the job of Residential Social Worker for young people (10-17 years old) turned out to be a different kettle of fish. The home was split into two units, both accommodating twelve residents, all with troubled family backgrounds, through both their own behaviour and that of their parents. Some needed protecting: with others it was the family!

The job entailed shift-work, each comprising a late shift (2-10pm), followed by an early (6am-2pm). Each week, a sleep -in would be required, making twenty-four hours on site. After Northampton, this was a baptism of fire; the skills I needed were still being refined, and on too many occasions I would find myself on the wrong end of an aggressive outburst by a resident - battered and bruised physically, and emotionally, too.

After two years, my resolve crumbled; unable to take the emotional rollercoaster, and not knowing how to unburden myself, I sought medical help, and after an initial month off work sick, it became a full nine months before I tried to return, but I was unable to continue. My spirit was crushed, and I left the job in August 1988.

A relationship, the first long-term one I had been in, came crashing to an end at the same time, compounding the loss of employment. Nothing appeared to raise my spirits or hopes. The faith that lifted a lost spirit inside in 1984 had disappeared, evaporated in the clouds of despair. For almost two years, life consisted of a twilight existence, full of drink and fishing.

Many years ago, I said that fishing is the worst drug of which I have ever partaken. 1988 saw the beginning of four years of self-neglect, lack of sleep, and becoming malnourished, yet thankfully I was rescued by a rebirth of the faith I had first found when at my lowest in 1984, and which was completed when I met Marie, my wife-to-be, in 1996; slowly, life balance and sanity were learnt - at times painfully - and maturity blossomed.

However, returning to the fishing in 1986!

Watford sits at one end of the Colne Valley, which was seen as the hub of British carp fishing. For all carp anglers, this was the place to be seen: 'The Waltonians', 'The Fisheries', 'The Rickmansworth Conservatives', 'Pit Four', 'Wraysbury One and Two', 'The Mere', 'Broadwater', 'Springwell'... the list could go on - were home to big carp - and for weeks on end, the anglers, too!

Even though the bug hadn't bit me yet, the magazines and weekly angling papers fanned my early yearning to chase these carp, too. However, for the first two years, fishing for tench and some of the smaller carp was where I wanted to be. I had enough pressure on time from work and trying to understand how to have a long-term relationship, which created a wedge between the fishing and my health.

As life started to unravel, solace was sought down on the bankside, usually Tolpits Lake, the nearest to home. I had joined Watford Piscators within months of moving, and had looked at the pit beforehand, as well as the other pits they controlled; the river and canal looked interesting, too.

My first trip to Tolpits saw me arriving with a pint of caster and a loaf of sliced bread. The swim chosen was appropriately named The Point, jutting out about twelve feet in front of the bungalow, a structure requiring some love and attention, where on June 15th every season the barbecue was held for the drawing of swims. The sloping margin of the swim, covered with lilies, made it look a great ambush spot for the tench.

The day had been warm and sunny; however, the temperature began cooling on arrival. Instinctively, I made the decision to fish at the bottom of the slope in nine feet of water, and for the first hour that is where a light waggler float sat, with a quarter of an inch proud above the flat calm of the surface; the wind had dropped to nothing after the breeze of the day. No bites were forthcoming, so while baiting with small balls of breadcrumb groundbait over the float, loose caster had been dropped at the top of the slope. The tench were not hungry; a few small roach and perch were seen scurrying about, and would give me some interest. All best intentions may change, however; when several tench moved onto the loose feed in two feet of water under my rod, they became the focus of attention. Not being slow in coming forward, I retrieved my tackle, and the problem became how to not spook them!

My chair was only five feet back from the water's edge; I feared that rearranging my position would make too much noise and disturbance, so the rod was held at a very high angle with the float dropped into the edge, after being reset to the shallower depth. From where I sat, the tench could been seen in the crystal-clear gravel-pit water, mouthing the caster or bread-flake bait. The first hooked fish only took a couple of minutes, a small fish of 2lb or so, and was followed by another eight in the next hour.

Twice a week, a visit was made to the pit; fishing in this manner in different swims resulted in similar catches, but I was setting up in a more comfortable position further back to allow the bait to be dropped next to the bank. However, in some of the deeper margins a nuisance fish created a fuss. On both baits, the carp, which at that time were not on the big-fish 'circuit', would be hooked once every trip. The tackle had been beefed up from a light float rod to the Terry Eustace Spec Nine rod I had built four years before, with a centrepin reel, loaded though with just 6lb line, which in hindsight wasn't really suitable or powerful enough.

But never once was the line snapped by a fight, even on the occasion when I felt a carp had run out of lake along the railway bank. I was sitting where the lilies ended, close to the bank, when the fish took the bait, screaming off along the margin to my right. Tree-roots were present for the complete length of the lake to the narrow end, which is where this fish headed. The distance was approximately fifty yards, and the centrepin just continued to spin. It was filled with around seventy-five yards of line, and when the fish stopped the spokes could clearly be seen under a few wraps of line. Holding onto the force of the run, the Spec Nine, in full battle-curve, sprung back sharply; winding the line back, I found the hook - an Au Lion d'Or - had slipped out of the fish's mouth.

The largest carp I landed in Tolpits on that tackle was 19lb 6oz, hooked on three casters on a size 12 hook, but larger were landed when my carp head was on, still a couple of years away.

In 1987, Watford Piscators took over the fishing rights on the Rickmansworth Aquadrome, consisting of Batchworth and Bury lakes. Everyone said Batchworth was the easier water; however, the carp only came out at night! For the first year, the carp stock appeared low; there was a head of large, high-backed commons, weighing to over 30lb. But the club, following the wisdom of Ben Tucker, head of their Water Management Committee, on which I sat a year or so later, stocked a large number of smaller mirrors. These fish, all between 6lb and maybe 10lb, soon packed on the weight, and were being caught on a regular basis. Even in the middle of winter, I had multiple catches of up to seven a night in temperatures of minus degrees C. Within a couple of seasons, the faster-growing carp were approaching high double-figures, and a year later the first 20-pounders appeared, but sadly the big original commons did a disappearing act.

This is where my transformation to carp angler started. In the first year, there was no matching tackle, so I made do with a

North Western 2lb test blank and the Spec Nine. By the time I moved on a year and a half later, a matching pair of Sportex 12ft Carbon Kevlar 2lb rods and Shimano Aerlex 4000's made me look the part. They rested on the Optonic bite-indicators, screwed into a double-head rod-rest, locked tight by gripper rests at the butt; both rods had to be parallel! One thing that was individual though, were the bobbins - instead of using monkey climbers or the recently introduced Hangers, mine were made from clear silicone tubing with a betalight slid inside, and a cocktail stick snapped in two with a black bead on the top, tensioned to hold the line in place. To adjust the amount of weight needed to tension the line, a link-swivel attached back to front allowed for a change in lead size, dependant on distance fished or requirements due to conditions. These bobbins, newly made, are still the type I use now in 2021.

Float-fishing was still my love, though; I would rather be creeping along the path, seeking carp mooching for morsels in the margin. Still using the Spec Nine and centrepin, but with a stronger line of 10lb, carp to nearly 20lb would regularly be caught. During this period, unbeknown to me, a nickname had been tagged onto me; it was a reference to my style of fishing as much as my appearance. My hair was still long, never having liked it short, and I would be seen creeping quietly around the lake, dropping a small bait, either casters, an 8mm boilie or a chickpea directly on the hook into the path of the carp cruising the margin. It is fascinating watching a carp mouth the bait, hardly moving a tiny piece of peacock quill; the float would not even break the surface film, remaining held by its tension, yet the fish had taken the bait back into its mouth. If time were counted off, the fish would pull the float under after fifteen seconds or so, but not from the fear a bolt-rig generates - it was moving to find another mouthful. The lesson here applied to legering, too; using the lightest lead possible, takes would be small movements. I received more of these than screamers in my time fishing for carp - and barbel in later years.

For my sins, the nickname 'Creeping Jesus', given to me by an unknown angler, made me feel proud; to me it meant at least others had noticed me. At first it was kept quiet; I didn't know about it until a few years after, when I was fishing Denham Pit 3. I would like to believe it was used as a term of endearment, but from the gossip heard from others, the name signified a negative response. I was supposed to be bending the rules, guesting on other pits, using banned baits - doing everything that might get me thrown off waters.

It makes me laugh now that I 'caught' fish I never caught, and my reputation went before me everywhere. Even twenty-five years after last fishing in the Valley, it would come back to haunt me! Shopping in the tackle shop in Bracknell during a lunch break from work, a conversation took place between me and a couple of other customers. No mention of the 'name' was made, so it was a surprise when I returned the next day and the shop owner took me to one side. His comment stayed with me for ages afterwards; he told me the other customers had asked him if he knew who I was? They told him, and said: "That's 'Creeping Jesus' - he used to be a good angler in his time!"

Used to be...! There were many more years to go; even a decade on, there is plenty of blood still to flow through these veins. There was another incident that made me laugh: in 2001, while fishing Ellis Lake in Shepperton, another angler stopped to chat. By this time, my long hair and beard had long since disappeared. As the conversation progressed, we found we had waters in common, and old stories were told. The other angler was in for a surprise, though; he brought up the name of 'Creeping Jesus', and all the things that angler was supposed to have done. I allowed him to continue for a few minutes before I politely asked him if he knew who he was talking to... His face was a picture as he gasped in embarrassment. The conversation ended suddenly, and he made an excuse before bidding me farewell.

CHAPTER THIRTEEN

BROADACRES - WATER MANAGEMENT

It eludes me now, but somehow I gained a place on the Water Management Committee of Watford Piscators. There was no experience to be drawn on, or skills that would help manage a fishery, so it will be put down to persistence and luck. Each member, apart from Ben Tucker, the head of the Committee, was assigned their own water. All were taken at the time, except a small pit at the end of the chain of five pits on the Tolpits site. Three were controlled by Watford: Tolpits, Stanley's Pool, and Broadacres on the opposite side of the canal. All could be night-fished except Broadacres, being inside the confines of the trout fishery there. The stock of the pit wasn't really of interest to the carp anglers, as they couldn't night-fish, and the other species weren't seen to be of worthwhile size; however, what put a lot of anglers off was the length of the walk required to reach the pit with all their tackle for a day's fishing!

So, I found myself taking care of Broadacres! Something I have found is that each venue tends to take on the personality or style of fishing of the person looking after it. With me it was no different; preferring a lake with tight little swims, hidden in the reeds, or having a small gap in the trees, Broadacres was left pretty much as I found it, with little tidying-up needed. Some of my friends jokingly commented that all the swims were left-handed, as they found it difficult to cast holding the rod in the right. I didn't say anything to contradict them!

Naming of swims helps in being able to keep concise records for future reference; a name in your logbook does give a label to the memory. However, the trap was fallen into quickly, and within days of seeing the water, I had named 'The Bay', 'The Gap', 'Big Canal', 'No. 4 Causeway', 'Entrance Corner', etc. All of them now have their own entries in my book, with captures to remember them by.

The task of tending Broadacres didn't really warrant much time or energy, not just because I liked it as it was, but because the club had no plans to stock it, or make big changes to the environment, so the status quo remained for the three years the water was under my watchful eye.

I fished more than ever; the excuse was to keep an eye out for trouble or poachers, but it was really because I fell in love with the atmosphere of the water, its moods, and its inhabitants, including the wildlife that would visit me, sitting quietly, soaking in the emotions given off from the history of the pit.

Broadacres is where bait-making first entered my fishing. The first attempts were undertaken using supermarket ingredients, while parallel to this my stepfather was using the same on the syndicate lake we belonged to in Cambridgeshire. The base was porridge oats; cheap and cheerful, it would bind well with the flavours, the peanut butter, milk, and egg-powders used for their protein. It could not be called a HNV Special, and the results were not great. It was not until my third season, and a switch to Premier Baits mixes with Fish Feed Inducing Oil at very low levels, that the fish started to come in numbers.

However, the cheap bait, made with a walnut oil and nut meals, did catch on the second season, producing my first twenty-pound-plus carp. By the beginning of September, I had only caught three carp, and it was not until the 10th that the next fish arrived in the net. Fishing the Gap swim over the next week, four more took a fancy to the bait. On the 16th, the afternoon session was coming to a close; having to be off the water half an hour after sunset, time had been pushed just 'a little past', when the bobbin on the left-hand rod moved a few inches and held against the rod. As I lifted the rod, the fish decided it wanted to be elsewhere, a fast run taking it over the bars in front of 'Arthur's', before turning down to the right and the 'Entrance'. Between me and the fish, a line of overhanging trees and thick roots threatened to bring the fight to a close. The fish had gone into the margin thirty yards away in the 'Entrance' swim, and wouldn't come out. Pumping it along under the trees, I feared it would snag up, but thankfully, after a few tense minutes, the fish was boiling under the rod-tip.

Ten minutes had passed since hooking the fish, and the fear of the trout fishery bailiff finding me on his after-dusk patrol was a real danger. I didn't want to bundle the fish into the landing net too quickly; she was co-operative, though, going into the mesh first time. Looking down at her, the realisation and the joy were enough for me to let out a stifled cry of delight. She was weighed at 25lb 10oz. Being by myself without self-take photographic equipment, she was returned without a fuss before I packed up and left the water without incident.

That was the last carp I caught that season, as I moved onto the River Gade to fish for chub. Trotting maggots produced nice bags of fish most trips, and it was warmer than just sitting wearing inappropriate clothing through a winter's carping.

The following year, Broadacres helped give me my first season of one hundred carp in a season - sixty-nine from Broadacres, the others spread around the Cambridgeshire syndicate, Wimblington, and even a couple from Tolpits in two days. It had started badly, and not until a change to the Premier fishmeal mix and low levels of Feed Inducing Oil, 5ml to three eggs, as bait, did things take off.

I hadn't fished Tolpits for a couple of seasons; my confidence was sky-high, and this boosted my opinion that I could catch from a harder water. Over the last two years, Tolpits had come to the notice of the carp circus; 'names' such as Terry Hearn and Jim Shelley had tried their hand on the water, and 30lb+ fish had come out.

Turning up to a very quiet lake on a September morning, the mist swirling over the lake surface and the sun slowly climbing above the tree-line on the Railway bank, all appeared dreamlike and surreal. It was one of those days when a sixth sense tingled within, a feeling that some of us may feel on magical days, when the stars align, and the god(s) are looking down on us. Chris Yates talks about it in his book 'Casting at the Sun'; others mention it in more hushed tones. It has been something I have been aware of on almost all those occasions when a special fish or multiple capture has occurred; not always, however, when distractions have silenced it, or the inner voice has spoken in a whisper.

Anyway, back to the day: walking slowly round to a swim on the Railway bank and setting up past the pads and a small bush, the cast could be placed on the leading edge of the lilies in twelve feet of water. My bait, the Premier mix with a low level of Fish Feed Inducing Oil that had caught almost all my fish during the last three months, was fished on a ten-inch 12lb Kryston Merlin hook-length. This was cast out with the aid of a 1oz lead, flicked sideways along past the bush; it landed spot on the point of the lily-bed, making a clean landing on gravel.

I placed the rod on the buzzer before walking around the bush to throw in a dozen loose boilies to attract the carp, and proceeded to set up the second rod, to be fished close into my right against a bush. Time of arrival had been 7.30am, and an hour and a half passed, sitting mesmerised, in a trance-like state, knowing something would happen. Without warning, the left buzzer screamed for attention; as I picked up the rod, it pulled aggressively round, and it was necessary to drop the rod-tip under the water to prevent the line catching in the branches of the bush.

The clutch of the reel had been set tightly, not wishing to give any line; it seemed ages, but it was only a minute or so before the fish headed out to open water in front of me. The water, being gin-clear, gave a clear view of a 20lb+ mirror twisting and turning, trying to evade capture. However, all went well, and she fell into the net first time.

She returned a weight of 24lb 8oz; a pleasing result, and worthy of a memory - unfortunately without the camera that day, it has to remain on the hard disk of my brain.

Broadacres produced the 25lb from the previous season on two more occasions, making the decision that it was time to move on easier. Its top weight in winter was 27lb 14oz on the 27th of January 1992.

Personal bests from four waters were the icing on the cake, but the thirty-pound barrier had not been reached. I was going through too much personal trauma, with the mental health difficulties from the residential work and the end of a loving relationship, to care much about breaking records, yet, unknown to my conscious self, the signs of obsession were bubbling, and were soon to erupt.

Broadacres holds fond memories of the friendships made there, and two have stood the test of time. Even with breaks through the years, whenever we meet or talk on the phone, it is still like yesterday, thirty years later. Paul Klinkenborg, who approached me to write my first-ever article for a magazine; his friend Tim Hodges had just started the magazine 'Carp Talk and Angling Techniques', and Paul suggested me as a contributor! The article was poorly written, and Paul, being a regular contributor to magazines, proof-read it and helped me, for which I am eternally grateful.

The other friend, Pete Clarke, nearly didn't become one - I was protective of Broadacres, and he was a new face. For an hour he stood talking with me, fishing in 'Arthur's', a swim where fish regularly topped - my insistence that there were not many fish in the lake fell on deaf ears as fish after fish began rolling over the first bar! We ended up fishing the afternoon together, getting on famously, and we still fish together now. We have been through many life changes, supporting each other and encouraging the other to keep on carrying on.

CHAPTER FOURTEEN

PIT THREE

After the success of 1991, a bigger challenge was needed. The thought of trying to gain entry into the more difficult clubs in the valley put me off somewhat, so a path of less resistance was chosen: the Gerrards Cross club-controlled Pit Three at Denham, a pit that lost out to its neighbours in the 'place to fish' stakes, while Pits Two and Four both saw a steady flow of anglers heading for their banks. On the other side of the Grand Union Canal running along the west side of the pit was Savay, and in Denham, Harefield, and other pits had more of a draw.

There was no waiting list to join Gerrards Cross, and the permit was within my finances, unlike most of the other clubs, who kept their membership to a limited and close-knit community. If your face didn't fit, or you lived too far from the Valley, there was no chance of obtaining a ticket for almost any pit, all having waiting lists filled with 'name' anglers wanting to get hold of one, sometimes at a price!

Gerrards Cross also ran a couple of stretches of the River Colne, so there was the chub fishing (I still had not put a barbel head on) in the winter, if needed to recharge the batteries. The pit was long and thin, about half a mile long, and two hundred yards at its widest. The stock level of carp at that time was around forty, a low density, making it a worthy challenge to overcome.

The previous year, I had read an article in the magazine 'Big Carp' by Dave Whibley, an account of a few days' fishing by the 'Famous Five' on the pit at the end of the 1990 season. The picture of a 28lb 8oz carp whetted my appetite, encouraging me to catch a fish or two from there.

The two seasons I spent fishing there were complete contrasts; during the first, all the fish came early, with none caught after July, while in the second season the fish - all bar one - came in March! A target was set for the first season of catching ten fish and five twenties; my confidence was not extremely high, but if you do not try you do not win. 'In for a penny, in for a pound' - it was worth an attempt.

June 16th saw me arriving at 3.30am. A walk or two to get to know the water had been undertaken the week before, and I knew where I wanted to fish. However, walking to a swim halfway down the far bank, where there was no car access, someone had beaten me to it! Retreating to another swim further back, some time was spent with a plumbing rod. I had plumbed other areas of the lake the week before, but not here. A plateau was found at sixty yards, rising out of much deeper water; this was a large expanse, going as far as I could cast.

No fish showed, and restlessness invaded my thoughts. With nothing better to do, a move was decided upon; this entailed a walk back to the car and a drive to the far end of the lake. An hour was spent looking at the water, trying to decide where to fish. I felt blind and lost, and eventually ended up on the other end of the 'blip'; a section of bank protruding out into the pit, thirty yards long and fifteen yards out into the water, where I had intended to fish in the first place.

The other angler was still in situ; however, he was covering water off to his left, so there would be no disturbance to each other. I did the polite thing, going over to ask if my position would affect his, to which he replied that it would not.

Setting up on a high bank to the left of a big bush hanging over the water, which could be seen to be shallow and weed-free, several casts were made with a marker rod to find a nice drop-off at twenty-five yards and a bar at forty, so my fishing positions were chosen. Some loose Premier baits were scattered by catapult over both spots, followed by two 11/2oz leads and hookbaits.

It must have been after midday when the first cast was made. Nothing had happened before Pete Clarke turned up, after a blank morning on the Waltonians. There was room for him to drop into a swim to my right; a social would pass the time.

Three hours quickly passed before I received a liner on the inside rod; this heightened the senses, and an hour later a drop-back signified a take. The fight wasn't hard; however, not knowing what was under the bush to the right gave me a few worrying moments, but no ill befell the battle and a small common of 18lb graced the net. To have caught on the first trip to a new water gave me the much-needed uplift of spirit - but little did I know what success was just around the corner.

A return trip the following day produced another common of 17lb 3oz; a different fish, as the one from the day before had no pectoral fin on the left side. This meant either I was doing it right, or just incredibly lucky!

While observing the water and waiting for another take, a couple of swans were seen feeding about fifty yards out from a swim off the far bank to my right. Knowing the water closer in there was twelve feet deep, this suggested to me an area to investigate, and the information was stored for the next trip.

Another Sixth-Sense Day!

Watercraft, some say, is learnt; others believe it is something we are born with - how to observe and learn from our environment, to treat it with respect as we partake in the nature of the waterside. Observing the swans six days before had put me onto a location that instinctively felt right; however, finding it took a couple of hours of constant casting from several swims before I successfully put a bait on it.

Driving under the railway bridge and passing the sailing club at the western end of the pit at 10.00am, it was a guessing game which swim the feature could be reached from. Taking the angle of eyeline from the swim on the far bank fished on the previous trip, I started in peg fifteen, about fifty yards from the start of the pit. Casting a plumbing rod set-up from here only found a constant depth and plenty of weed. A move was made two swims up, and the process was repeated there - again with no joy.

After two more leapfrog moves along the bank, the feature was found in front of the swim with the first cast. The plumbing float had been cast about sixty yards to find seven feet of water; pulling it back one pull of the rod gave a depth of two feet, and on the next it had dropped back to four. Continuing the process twice more, the line plunged off a cliff-face into a depth of over twelve feet.

There appeared to be little weed on top of the eight-yard-wide plateau; there was, however, a nice clean gravel bottom.

Feeling confident that this was the spot the swans had been feeding on, the decision was made to loose-feed lightly over the shallow area before the rods were set up. Time had crept by, and the first cast wasn't made until 12.30pm.

Time ticked slowly by; sitting in a pleasant, sunny heat of 20C. with a North-Westerly breeze blowing from left to right - all was right with the world. Confidence was bubbling up within me, with both rods placed on the plateau: the left one at the back in two feet of water and the right in six feet before the drop-off.

1.05pm: the left-hand rod signalled a stuttering take, the bobbin holding and gently rocking below the rod. Lifting into the fish, the expected reaction still took me by surprise, as a massive tail surfaced before the reel went into meltdown. The fish took forty yards of line from the reel before the pressure slowed the run, and a process of pumping the fish back towards me drew it down into the deeper water, where it plodded about. It took several minutes before the fish started to rise enough to be seen. An apparition rose through the depths - a big mirror carp; immaculate in its beauty, it slid over the waiting rim of the forty-two-inch landing net, where I left her, getting scales and unhooking mat ready before bringing her ashore.

Never having caught a fish so large, I was breathless, my heart racing inside my chest. Lifting her up onto the unhooking mat, the weight - unprepared for - released the childlike joy within to make me smile insanely. However, pulling myself together, the weighing produced a figure of 30lb 5oz, my first ever 30lb+ carp. However, not everything went my way; fifty minutes later, a take on the right-hand rod found a thick weed-bed, and even leaving the rod for an hour, a loss had to be accepted.

The action slowed until 5.15pm, when another take to the left rod produced a 26lb 9oz mirror, followed an hour later by another to the same rod at 22lb 0oz. This was my first experience of a catch of such magnitude; nowadays, if we believe the angling press, catches like this are ten a penny, the number of pits and lakes stocked with much bigger specimens having superseded them, yet at the time, it was a catch of dreams for most anglers.

Not being an angler who hides his captures, I told my fishing companion Pete Clarke as soon as I returned home in the evening. We didn't have mobile phones then; the grapevine was much slower, relying on landline phones or sharing stories down the pub. I told him what swim, positions of bait, etc, and he said he would have a go the following day. I had to work in the morning, so arranged to visit him later.

On arrival, I was surprised to find Pete in the swim to the right of my swim from the previous day. Tackle wasn't going to be taken, but it had been put in the car anyway. To cut a long story short, Pete had caught two small tench during the day; I fished for an hour and a half in the swim and caught another big carp of 28lb 8oz. The 30-pounder would see the bank twice for me over the two seasons I spent fishing the pit. On the first occasion, the picture was taken lying on the unhooking mat; fortunately, at the last capture in March of the second season, someone was fishing a swim close by and came to take the pictures.

The weight of the winter capture is suspect, as my 32lb Avon scales bottomed out; even after dialling them as far round as they would go, giving another 2lb, they still would not take the full weight. The other angler was insistent, though, that the fish was 32lb 0oz, and he wouldn't bring his larger scales to reweigh her. I still didn't chase glory, so I accepted his figure, yet nowadays I do still wonder what the true weight should be...

Over the two seasons, I fished no more than four hundred hours both seasons. Much of the time was spent looking across the pit and at motionless bobbins hanging below a pair of rods

sitting parallel on the buzzers. Would I have caught more stalking? It will never be known, but a total of fifteen carp for 359lb 15oz is not a bad result.

The following year, the controlling club stocked more carp and the fishing changed. I was glad to be heading for pastures new - Rickmansworth Conservative Club here I come.

CHAPTER FIFTEEN

THE CONSERVATIVES - THE BIG LEAGUE

I had hoped my two years on Denham Pit Three would have prepared me for the 'Big League'. The two lakes of 'The Cons', as it was known, held many more large carp, and the anglers who fished for them put faces to the names read in the angling press. Who was I to believe it would be possible to live up to their standards - would they just laugh at this interloper pretending to be a carp angler?

Getting into the club, an angler had to go through an interview with the twelve members of the committee. You had to have been proposed by a member, who in my case was Pete Clarke, the friend made on Broadacres and companion on Pit Three. He had been a member on the Cons. and other pits such as the Harrow Waltonians for many years, accepted in the ranks of the elite; however, he was not as aloof as many of the other anglers, and for that I am thankful.

The queue slowly moved ahead of us; there were a least another twenty other anglers attempting to gain membership, but finally it was my turn before the committee. It felt how I would imagine standing in front of the Spanish Inquisition would be; the feeling of fear that I felt, a naughty schoolboy waiting to be caned by the headmaster. Pete was asked to speak first, to give his character reference. There was an air of bemusement within the room when upon being asked the first question, "Was I a carp angler?", I informed them I only fished day sessions and didn't own a bivvy or a bedchair!

After what felt like an eternity, the questioning was over; amazingly, I had been accepted for membership, but the fishing had to wait! There was a rule that new members could not fish until the first week in July, to give the existing members a chance to catch a few before the stampede and overcrowding a new influx brings. This was not a deterrent; it gave me more time to prepare and convince myself it would be OK on the night - the curtain would not fall to end the play before it had started.

The 2nd of July was the first occasion I arrived with tackle, more to get to know a few swims on the large lake than anything else. The small lake would be left for later, when I had proved to myself my fishing would hold up to the competition! No fish were seen to be caught that evening, so on my return the following afternoon, the excitement of a new water still filled the air. I had arranged with Pete to meet him on the lake; arriving first, the decision was made to set up on the right-hand side of the Point; however, when Pete turned up, he opted to fish the left side. Moving in next to him, we both fished close in over the lily-pads, which seemed the right idea. Pete was first off the mark with a 23lb mirror, followed an hour later by my 'virgin' fish, a 24lb 8oz common, getting me off the mark. It came to my usual tackle and bait set-up, as I saw little need to change.

As with Pit Three, I hit the ground running, and landed another three fish in the next week. The catch rate did slow, as the lake sulked after the initial onslaught of the season, and the carp did a disappearing act - except for those anglers prepared to get up early and move onto fish. As a day angler, this put me at a disadvantage, as the lake, packed as it was, meant I had only a small chance of turning up and getting a going swim. The few times I did, a capture would occur. One day in September, I managed three fish in an afternoon, fishing off the end of the Point, casting to the back of the lilies in front of the 'Piggery' swims.

By winter, catches had dried up for everyone; I didn't see a single carp between 17th October and 11th March - both my captures. I was glad to see the end of the season, yet was hopeful for the following season, when I could start on the 16th of June, with the other seasoned members!

Blinded by Love

The pattern of the second season followed the first, in that fish came quickly. By the end of the first week, I had landed three carp; however, a change was on the way! During late April, I had met Marie, and had become bewitched, falling head over heels for her beauty. The need to spend so much time at the lake decreased - I even missed the first two days of the season, spending time in Somerset with her.

Not much fishing was done throughout the whole season; our lifestyle allowed for several foreign holidays, and our involvement with the church took up time. This was a new experience, only having had one long-term (lasting less than a year) relationship in my life, and commitment needed to be learnt. The feeling that at long last, at the age of thirty-nine, maturity had caught up with me; the need to be selfish and seek solitude became less of an issue. Till then I had protected myself, not giving anyone the chance to get close; female, and even male, friends, had been kept at arm's length. At the first sign of emotional trouble, I would duck and dive, running for cover as far away as possible. The lakeside or riverbank gave me this opportunity; talking to someone else became my choice, and more likely the choice was made not to.

Acknowledging that the tunnel vision followed in a relationship is no more intense than the behaviour associated with an obsession, and fishing, does create the same actions in us; everything we do and say is about fishing, unless there is a conflict of interest. The battle of the desires to follow both may

be bloody and painful as we are drawn in two directions, both crying out for our attention. Whichever wins becomes dominant; we are at the mercy of its every whim. The obsession is not the individual, though; it is the emotion we feel - Marie was not the obsession; it was what the relationship would offer that led me away from the lake for almost the complete season.

The only other trip made to 'The Cons' came a week before the end of the season, on the 5th of March. Fittingly, the trip produced a common of just under 20lb, becoming my last fish from the lake. I had made the decision once again to move on; having physically moved further away from the lake, the search started to find a lake or two nearer to my new home.

CHAPTER SIXTEEN

A NEW HOME TO HANG MY HAT

August 23rd, 1997: Marie and I married; fishing was still on the back burner, but I wasn't really missing it - our lives were full of the pleasures and trials of a new life together. As with every couple, young or old, gaining an understanding of the other person's needs and wants brought the good times and sometimes bad; however, there was a determination to win through in both parties.

Not only had our relationship taken a big part in my life, the previous summer, a university degree course in Social Work also beckoned for attention. This put strain on the budding relationship, as I was only working part-time for a Social Work agency, requiring waking night shifts in homeless hostels, being away from home at weekends, and undertaking residential shifts as far from home as Milton Keynes.

The burden this placed on Marie and me could have been too much, yet we survived, growing ever stronger as a couple. However, my mental health did suffer; depression bit at my heels - as Winston Churchill described it, his 'Black Dog' - and haunted my thoughts. In a relationship, the couple tell each other there will not be any secrets; but this was mine - I tried to hide my insecurity and fear of failure, and not until maybe five years on did I give a name to my behaviour for Marie to try and understand.

Man tries to conquer every mountain, cross every torrent, and beat his opponent as quickly as he can; not, as we may believe, to say: 'Look at how good I am', but to cover up our insecurities and fears. Our biggest fear is to be seen as a failure - the 'big boys don't cry' mentality. We want to be the hunter, the provider, yet inside we quiver with fear that we will not bring home the meal or provide a roof over the family's head.

I needed to find a space to call my own, and fishing offered this, but it would eat into even more time that I needed to spend with Marie - until a compromise was made, which means meeting each other where the other is, not giving something up as the world sees, the pressure grew. We agreed that fishing wouldn't take place at weekends, which suited me fine, never having been a fan - too many other anglers out fishing, and fish when Marie was at work.

Moor Lane

Knowing I only had brief periods of time, a small local lake met my needs. Run by Kingsmoor Angling, Moor Lane lake, a small couple-of-acres pool, became home from home once or twice a week. Being small enough, it suited a float-fishing approach, and particles fished under a small quill lift-method style gave sport from mainly mid-double-figure carp.

As with all lakes or rivers, there is always a lost fish story, and here was no different! Float-fishing a small cube of luncheon meat in the narrow bottom corner, with a 1.25 test curve rod and centrepin reel, the float suddenly shot away; the expected carp metamorphosed into a black tail slapping the surface, and an amazing turn of speed. The lake held a couple of catfish of about 20lb, and this was one of them. The expected happened: burying itself in the thick weed, the chance of landing it decreased, and the line came back limp, having been cut off by an unseen snag.

Marie had always said she would come fishing; a hot September afternoon a fortnight after returning from our honeymoon, a bottle of wine in the tackle-bag and a magazine for her to read, we drove the mile to the lake for a few hours. I picked a rather tight swim; the weed reached the surface only a rod-length out, leaving very little water to cast to. Thinking it was just nice to be out fishing with Marie, I was not deterred. Placing a peanut bait on the left against the bush, and a small boilie to the right, both on lead set-ups and buzzers, we sat back to soak up the sun.

We had arrived at 12.45pm, casting the first bait at 1.00pm; nothing was expected, if at all, until it cooled down later in the afternoon. So, when the left-hand rod screamed off at 1.30pm, I was surprised, to say the least. It gave a short fight, with me holding the fish tight against the bush, before it rolled into the landing net.

At 21lb 6oz, even Marie looked excited, but foolishly I made the mistake of upsetting her by laughing, when she innocently exclaimed: "You have caught one now, can we go home?"

Marie did come fishing with me a few more times over the next few years; however, the trip to Sivyers Lake on a warm, windy evening would be her last. Setting up to float-fish on the windward bank, our nostrils didn't pick up the smell at first; it was Marie who noticed it, commenting on the foul smell that must be coming from somewhere near us. Standing up and looking into the water by the bush at the edge of the swim, Marie found the cause of the stench: the corpse of a small carp that had blown in on the wind, and lay decomposing in the margin.

Unfortunately, my float lifted while she was showing her distaste for the choice of swim, resulting in a 19lb common, making it difficult for me to be persuaded to move swims. However, after a short 'adult discussion' – or disagreement - I unwillingly moved further along the bank. A couple more reasonable carp were landed, but Marie had a long face all evening, complaining about the wind in our faces. On return to our home, Marie politely informed me that she would not come fishing ever again; she has kept her word.

The River Thames

Living in Staines, the River Thames flowed close to our home. The walk to a fishable bank was no more than a quarter of a mile; passing the 'The Bells' public house and St Mary's church, a turn into Riverside Close brought you out onto a short stretch leading to the Sea Cadets HQ and beyond to where the River Colne flowed into the Thames a hundred yards downstream, or, by crossing the bridge, it was possible to fish outside the Ship Hotel. All these spots produced fish, but I was unlucky to not hook any of the larger carp that were seen in the Colne during the close season, spawning a few hundred yards upstream. The biggest, a known leather carp, came out at 38lb+, and would have made me a very happy man -and so would the two that were even bigger!

However, the Thames carp would have to wait for another time; already, unbeknown to me, the obsession was waning, and it would not be until barbel became my new love; that the River Thames saw my rods again.

CHAPTER SEVENTEEN

PUTTING MY 'BIGGER FISH' HEAD ON AGAIN

By 1998, I was into my third year at university, attempting to achieve an improvement on the education gained at school - I had left with three 'O'- levels by the skin of my teeth, having to re-sit them at a college of further education. The course chosen, a degree in Social Work, had not gone to plan - being an opinionated person, the art of following the party plan – giving a tutor what they wanted in your essay - was not easy for me.

Jumping before I was pushed, I transferred to another course, Social Sciences, at the end of the first year; this saw a great improvement in my grades, and even subjects that overlapped both courses, and had been marked down, now resulted in high marks!

But the strain of not bringing in a full-time wage to cover my share of the household bills had started to affect my mental health. Not being the provider that man expects of himself, I put pressure on myself to find a job that would help. Knowing this would make the possibility of full-time study and travelling to Hatfield in Hertfordshire five days a week difficult, it would require considering going part-time.

In discussion with Marie, this was the path chosen, so the quest began. The job-search took a bit more time than envisaged, not finding one until early 1999. I started to work for a Housing Association in the role of Housing Support Worker in Mental Health. The job was in Hemel Hempstead, so it still required travelling around the M25; a small sacrifice to make, if ends were to meet.

Starting part-time study appeared to lift the mental pressure off me; fishing had to take a back seat again, compromise if needs must. I continued in this role for eight years; however, the pressure and study became too much; I needed to seek medical support for the second time in my life, and a course of anti-depressants were prescribed. The choice of what is most important in a life came to the fore; the male ego was being tested and flexed.

Does a man have to be a provider, bringing in a wage to support the family; does he have to be an emotional support to his wife; or does he need to prove to the world he can achieve, and pass the examinations? The decision was easier than imagined - job, degree, or wife, there was no choice to be made - I decided my marriage was the most important. Continuing to work, I walked away from the university course only one module before having sufficient marks to gain a degree.

Some would say it was foolhardy, others may believe it brave - I was given a university diploma; not enough to climb the professional ladder - however, working on the ground floor in social services can be more rewarding, still working with individuals, not pushing numbers and finance.

There was no pounding of a heavy heart, no anxiety as to whether I had done the right thing, only a relaxed peace - and ironically, a freedom to enjoy fishing again, which led to a return to chasing big carp on new waters, giving me the much-needed kick up the bottom!

Looking at Ordnance Survey maps of the area surrounding Staines, the choice of water was overwhelming: the gravel pits in the Colne Valley, the pits on the opposite bank of the River Thames at Sunbury and Shepperton, and of course the Thames itself, all gave the opportunity to catch big carp. Where did I start?

The pits in Wraysbury seemed an obvious starting point, but I was led to look at Shepperton and the Sheepwalk pits controlled by Feltham Angling Club. Both could be fished on a day-ticket, giving open access to explore, and only a fifteen-minute drive from home - venues that would be available for short sessions before or after going to university or work.

The first trip was made on a cold, miserable March morning in 1998. Parking outside the gate, the view of the smaller pit greeted me. The weather conditions gave it an air of lifelessness; nothing moved on the water's surface except a cold North-Westerly breeze, cutting through my winter coat.

The pit had a surface area of about four acres, making the walk round easy and relatively short. A choice of swim had been made on the top bank, with an open view of almost the whole of the pit. I was in no hurry that day; it was an exploratory visit. A half-hour's plumbing soon located a bar at thirty-five yards, rising to ten feet out of sixteen; behind was a nice silty patch, and the bar was covered in gravel.

My bait a new one sourced from Jim Rawcliffe of 'Tails Up Baits' (the firm is now run by someone else; however, Jim now has a company called 'More Takes'). During a visit to his shop, where he rolled his baits, an interesting conversation had given me an insight into his philosophy on the making of baits, and made me very happy to purchase a bait or two. Today's was a Provit Liver, in 14mm size.

Placing the marker float on top of the bar, it was used as a sight to cast to. One rod cast close to it, followed by the second, cast to the back of the bar - the waiting game began. Having arrived at 6.00am, it had taken until 7.00am to sort myself out. Much of my time fishing at that time was spent reading or making notes for essays for the university course still being studied at Hatfield - using the time constructively, but when a take came, it caused problems, and many a time the paper or book would be dropped into thick, clinging mud. As the books had been brought home from the university library, they would require cleaning before being taken back, delaying my journey if they needed to be returned that day!

Today was no different: when the take came, the books were thrown down, and I reached for the left-hand rod fished onto the bar as the bobbin hit the rod and the buzzer screamed to a 'one-toner'. Size was not important; the first fish from any lake is a joy, and coming so quickly, it encouraged me - I was on the right track.

Over the next three months, I continued to fish the small pit; however, after walking around the large pit, the bigger fish seen distracted me, and I soon had my bait in the deep, clear water attempting to catch them.

During May of the same year, many of these carp made their way down to the motorway corner, a shallower area of the pit, snag-ridden yet fishable; I set up with the rod-tips pushed to the gravel bottom to camouflage the line. A bait was placed only ten feet from the rod-tip, where fish were feeding over the hemp and a few boilies. A 1oz lead to keep disturbance to a minimum

was lowered gently into the swim, at a moment when the fish had drifted back into the bushes to my right. Only fifteen minutes later a take came, resulting in a 25lb 4oz common.

During the rest of May, the fish managed to disappear, and a search was undertaken high and low. To make it harder, the whole pit was almost one massive weed-bed; even in depths of over twenty-three feet, the weed reached the surface, and there were very few clear spots to be found, most being in the margins.

Frustration could have taken over; throwing in the towel seemed easier, but not being one to give in, my search continued. The 17th of June, a day to be forgotten - one of those "I hooked one so big...", a loss that has stayed with me till now, and will stay with me until my dying day. The adversary was not seen, only felt; I described it as though a lawn roller, one of the old-fashioned, very heavy hand-pushed monstrosities, was rolling down a hill and I was trying to stop it - yet it kept on rolling!

The cast had been made from a swim I called 'The Tunnels', on the opposite bank from the inflow and Channel swims thirty yards across the bay. No one else was fishing, meaning a cast into the inflow became possible. The margin in the small bay of the inflow had only approximately three feet of water; it was a hard cast, as I had to kneel to cast under the trees in the swim above my head, and the lead hit the spot first time. The light bobbin sat three inches from the rod, swaying gently in the breeze, awaiting the take.

It was a hot, sunny day, lulling me into a dozy half-sleep, broken by the beeps from the buzzer at midday - the bobbin had crept to the rod and held. Upon striking, a solid, immoveable resistance held its ground for several seconds before moving out into open water. The 3lb test curve Harrison Ballista rod locked over into its full battle-curve; the line cut into the water's surface, moving at a snail's pace - no movement was felt, just the sense that a living creature was on the end.

No clicking of the reel's drag could be heard; the rod kept being pulled down, parallel to the water, and slackening off the drag appeared to do nothing. If speed could be measured, I doubt if the fish moved at more than 2mph as it swam away, covering about ninety yards before it stopped. Knowing the swim, I remembered with alarm that a bird platform twenty yards down the left margin had submerged in the recent past, and was still supported by the thick chain, ten feet off the bottom.

The fish allowed itself to be pumped back towards the swim; however, the path being taken led straight to the sunken platform. The bushes between it and my swim did not allow for any change of angle - a collision course had been set. The fish charged back into open water, alleviating the danger but only putting it off.

Eventually, the fish approached the chain, and anticipating the outcome, I stepped into the margin; water lapped around my chest; rod locked, and reel tightened, an act of desperation had to be put in operation, so the bail-arm was taken off and slack given, hopefully to encourage the unseen leviathan to move away. Unfortunately, everything went solid, so the rod was placed back on the buzzer, the bail-arm back on with a slackened drag, praying for a miracle that didn't happen. Two hours - still nothing had happened; I pulled for a break, but with 15lb Big Game, it was harder than you would think. We all wonder at 'the one that got away'; well, images of the 3lb test curve rod being pulled parallel to the water are imprinted on the hard drive of my memory. In a way, I was glad the fish never showed itself - knowing how big it was would only have made it worse.

During the following year, several fish were landed up to 28lb; it became a struggle, and to keep my head in gear, trips to another Feltham water, Sivyers, a 'runs' water, regularly produced fish up to 19lb 4oz and put a smile on my face when needed.

Wanting to keep on after a bigger fish led to moving no more than ten yards from the top bank of Large Sheepwalk; on the other side of the fence, a 130-acre pit called Ellis, a Civil

Service-controlled water, had whispered my name, casting a spell through the carp seen to be captured. It was hard fishing; most fish hooked were landed from a boat, and almost exclusively, baits and feed were boated out over a hundred yards to clear spots.

However, the spell cast seemed not to be working, as no carp came my way for two years, though tench a-plenty up to nearly 8lb saw the landing net. I only hooked one carp, on the last trip fishing in the lagoon. The decision had already been made to move elsewhere, and losing this fish only encouraged the move to pastures new.

CHAPTER EIGHTEEN

THE QUEEN'S BACK GARDEN - VIRGINIA WATER

What triggered the memory of a particular friend, I am not sure. We had fished together in 1988, both seeking close season sport at Farlows, pretending to catch trout on boilie, maggots, and bread! The previous year, the government had passed a law to allow close season coarse fishing on stillwaters stocked with trout. Some clubs and day-ticket waters quickly jumped on the bandwagon, Farlows being one of the first. Boyer's, the gravel company that owned the lake, stocked a few other lakes as well.

I had been fishing at Farlows a few months before Chris and I met. Until then, my fishing consisted of maggots under a float in the margins, catching tench and bream and hooking carp, landing the majority. Fancying a change, parking at the small gate next to the M25 corner, it was a short walk to the reed-fringed bay, which offered sport with small carp galore. Still fishing a float cast across to the reeds, another angler joined the fun, fishing a similar method a little down the bank.

We introduced ourselves, and spent the day enjoying the company, agreeing to meet up again later in the week. This friendship grew as we travelled to fish other waters together, as far away as Broadlands in Hampshire. However, after three years, a disagreement drew us in different directions, finally parting on bad terms without a goodbye.

I rarely thought of Chris, until I saw him on the front page of an angling paper, having caught a 50lb common carp from a southern water. Looking through my address book, his number hadn't been taken out, and living nearer to Windsor where he lived, the risk was taken to try and see if he would speak to me. Only a few weeks later, we met in the 'Bells' public house for a drink and a catch-up. Both of us had been through much change in our lives; I had married, while he had left work due to serious health difficulties and separated from his wife.

Some friendships are able to reconnect and carry on as though there hadn't been a break - this appeared to be one of them! The talk turned to fishing, and what we wanted from it; both of us admitted to being drawn to fish the large lake in Windsor Park, that is Virginia Water.

A lake with four-and-a-quarter miles of bank space - at that time there was no fishing on the northern bank, and no parking near the areas of the lake we preferred to fish, so it was a long walk to most of the swims. Chris, though, ever a thinking man, brought himself a fold-up bike and had a purpose-made trolley for the back on which fitted his tackle; I would walk as fast as I could alongside him with my barrow.

The decision to pre-bait felt essential; on such a large expanse of water, the fish needed to be held by feed to stay in the areas chosen to fish. Approaching 'Tails Up Baits' and Jim Rawcliffe, a deal was struck at a good price, which saw us purchasing over a hundred kilograms of 'Far Eastern' boilies, and more were bought to use as bait later in the season.

The burden of pre-baiting fell on Chris; he would cycle from his home in Windsor for his daily exercise early every day, carrying five kilos of bait and a spod rod to lay a carpet of loose-feed. Never had I been involved with a big pre-baiting campaign; what little I did, three visits a week with a catapult and two kilos, was just a top-up.

The season dawned; arriving at the Black Nest end of the lake soon after Chris, an air of expectancy hung over the water. With me walking beside him, setting a pace faster than normal, the chosen swims were reached. We had made the decision to bait-up a narrow arm, leading under the bridge spanning the road that led into the park. The arm continued, ending at what was called the Chinese temple, but there was no evidence of a temple in 2001.

At the entrance, a cast of nearly one hundred yards was required to reach the lily-beds spreading along the far-bank margin. These had been baited up five days a week for a month, with almost all the bait bought from Jim. Our enthusiasm became overwhelming, knowing we would catch, yet it took several hours before the first fish hit the spreader block of Chris's landing net.

A small common of about 7lb, coming to three grains of maize fished half-way across and off the feed, made us question our motives for pre-baiting, but we need not have worried. By midday, both of us had caught several commons, the biggest just into double figures.

The first day's results, as in the following few weeks, proved to us that the majority of the stock were these smaller commons; we caught up to ten a day between us, from this area and subsequent swims all season. The bigger fish, both commons and mirrors, did not appear till the next year.

Moving to other areas of the lake, fishing took place from the top end of the Eastern arm at the Totem Pole, to the inlet at the Black Nest end, and everywhere in between. Even though we knew individuals were breaking the rules and entering the park at night to fish in the copse near the ruins, we stuck to the daylight hours. At £55 a season, it was value for money, and knowing our captures were honest made it even more worthwhile.

Our last season fishing together, the third on the lake, produced the biggest fish; a move to the middle of the lake to the swim we called the 'Wides' gave us fish up to my best for the lake at 28lb 12oz. There were bigger present, yet did it matter anyway?

My larger fish always came on a day when fishing alone, and still not owning a camera suited for self-takes, no pictures were taken.

The only picture from three years fishing the water, a 20lb 12oz common.

CHAPTER NINETEEN

CHERTSEY LANE AND KINGSMEAD ONE

If nothing else, three years spent fishing Virginia Water had taught me that there was no enjoyment in fishing a big water; it required time I was unwilling to spare, and the need to return to the small, intimate lakes - or even ponds - ate away at my resolve. The yearning to be creeping amongst the foliage and undergrowth, being stung by nettles and scraped by brambles, beckoned, drawing out the masochist in me, the pain inflicted resulting in the pleasure of the capture.

On the local grapevine in Staines, there were whispers of a small pit on the road to Chertsey that held large carp. The search did not prove too difficult; quickly locating both the pit and the controlling club, membership was obtained a week before the new season started.

The pit was small even by my standards, covering an area of less than half an acre. One island sat close to the bank opposite the car park, creating a beautiful, deep channel of eleven feet to ambush carp. Most of the pit was shallow, under six feet, and was covered by large weed-beds; however, enough clear spots were available to float- fish in between them.

Carp were easy to observe; most days they would be seen cruising close to the weed, and none I saw weighed less than 20lb. My choice of tackle consisted of a Wychwood 1.75lb test curve barbel rod and a Grice and Young centrepin reel, loaded with 12lb Big Game line.

Through observation, it was noticed that the carp had a preference to feed on sweetcorn. All the other anglers fished in a rigid fashion, with matching rods and boilies, giving me the opportunity to take advantage of a bait and method - float fishing - without hopefully making the carp too wary.

Fish started to come on my infrequent visits; I was still fishing elsewhere, feeling that the pit would be a hard nut to crack, and sanity needed to be preserved. The break from using matching tackle on medium-sized pits was still a draw, and Kingsmead One on the Leisure Sport ticket fulfilled this need.

However, in my eyes, the strain of carp to be found in Kingsmead left a lot to be desired in terms of beauty, and their short, plump bodies appeared so unnatural compared to the fish I was used to. My enjoyment and pleasure soon waned, bringing to the fore a feeling, an emotion, that not only was my enjoyment for this pit not there, but it also faded in the gloom, as obsession lost its hold.

Not even the capture of a personal best from Chertsey Lane of 33lb 5oz, caught on float tackle, could fan the flames again. Other emotions rained on my parade; would life ever be the same?

TIMES HAVE CHANGED AND
THE LOVE HAS GONE

March 2006

As the sun set on the last day of the season, packing up saddened my soul and my mind became blank - at that moment, I knew the affair had ended. Since 1986, almost all my time at the waterside had been spent fishing for carp, with many memories from many lakes, yet as a lover I felt dejected and hurt. I am not blaming my lover (the carp); no, I blame myself: my actions were selfish, my needs were important, always wanting more - a bigger fish, more fish in a day... Did I really care at all? I came home thinking: "Does it matter anyway...?"

Do I want to feel the fire again, or do I need to go away to recharge the batteries? Is it that important to catch a 40lb+ carp; is it worthy of all the time I have not got? Until a few years ago, time was on my side - I believe that it still is; however, I don't make it work for me anymore. Instead of being at the lake looking, talking, or baiting and plumbing, I spend time moaning and moping around, blaming everyone else (the wife, or lack of time – work!).

2008

There were occasions when the feelings returned briefly; the start of June 2008 being a prime example. Having joined a new club with the intention of fishing their river stretches for barbel, I found myself wandering the banks of a couple of the lakes, wondering what to do. Within five minutes, I had stumbled upon a group of large carp feeding in the margins, and further along the bank another group... Now, not being slow on the uptake,

I rushed home to get my carp float rod, centrepin reel and bait. I spent four hours of enjoyable stalking without a fish on the bank that evening; next day, however, a 26lb common on the bank within forty minutes of arriving made the embers glow.

Over the next three weeks, I spent several short sessions in other areas of the lake with two lead rods, and caught another smaller common, which pulled the rod from my hand as soon as the bait hit the bottom twenty-five feet out. A couple of 8lb tench also came my way; somehow, though, I could not keep up the enthusiasm. The lust of the blossoming new affair withered and died when I realised the lakes in question asked more than I could give. The lover asked for commitment, and I was unable to give it, or at least the amount of time required to give the attention the lover desired.

When approaching the larger, low-stocked waters that had been my fishing home for many years (and this new water was fifty acres, with a reasonably low stock level), there is a requirement to spend plenty of hours at the water, not only fishing but getting to know it. Many would have said I was lucky, finding the fish so quickly; I would agree - however, I would like to believe that many years of water-craft give an advantage in knowing the best areas to look at first.

So, what is more important, catching carp or our other life with friends, family, and human lovers? I did not have the answers; I chased the ideal of trying to balance both, but the fishing lost more than ever. Was I happy with this? I felt as though the drug I was addicted to had been removed and I was suffering constant cold turkey, withdrawal leaving me in a cold sweat.

In 1996, I wrote in an article that fishing was the worst drug I had ever used (and in my youth I was dependant on many), and I still hold to this. At its worst, an angler does not eat well, sleep enough; he self-neglects and is anti- social.

I was working in the community with individuals suffering from mental health difficulties (which, if we believe the statistics, one in four of all of us will suffer from in life), seeing individuals with heavy dependence on both legal and illicit drugs to cope with life, and the results are, in some cases, not that different. The battle for the ideal of having it all puts pressure upon a man, as does each struggle to justify his selfishness while seeking that ultimate goal. Angling should be a pleasurable pastime, but when it becomes your *life*, it is an addictive drug.

Book Three
The barbel years:

Waiting for the reel to scream

REPRISE - TIMES HAVE CHANGED
AND THE LOVE HAS GONE

2009 All change, and lust kicks
in again – Barbel, a new lover!

During the winter of the 2008/09 season, I visited a local stretch of the River Kennet for the first time, and in two trips I managed a 9lb fish first time out and two of 10lb 6oz and 8lb on the second. Both trips were short afternoon sessions on a flooded river; however, the thrill of hooking these fish, which gave a good account of themselves, relit the fire of love - or was it lust? - the warmth of the passion of orgasm in the fresh embrace of capture.

At the start of the next season, I had become immersed in the new relationship. In celebration, my brother Jeff booked two days on the Royalty's compound weir for my fiftieth birthday (belatedly). Walking onto the 'hallowed' ground on the 7th July 2009, I felt as though I had been taken home to meet my love's parents: nervous, heady, and scared I would make a fool of myself. The fish could have responded better; however, going home with three to my name gave me the feeling of satisfaction that I had been accepted as one of the family.

Lust does not last forever, and two years into the relationship it had settled into the realms of a marriage. I doubt if I am the only barbel angler who has felt this way. At its best, my love comes to greet me as soon as I arrive at the desired swim. How many occasions has the tip flown around within seconds of placing the rod on the rests? My personal best at the time, at 15lb 9oz, caught on 28th November 2009, came on such an occasion, leaving me with the feeling of "where do I go from here?" The heady rush of joy in the capture, the pleasure of the kiss of her head in the net... At worst, my love will turn her back on me, or sulk after an argument, not letting me close to comfort, not responding to my love, making me feel rejected and pained. Most of the time it is going through the motions of the mundane, buying the bait and tackle, cleaning up after dinner, treating her to a meal out (well, the best bait money can buy!).

However, it does not matter how my love treats me; I return time and time again, walking the riverbanks searching her out, looking in the gaps in the weed-beds for a glimpse of her bronzed beauty. A reflection of glinting gold lying in the fold of my mat, gazing into her eye; the time spent sitting waiting patiently for her to respond; going home after a fishless day, knowing her mood will change again.

CHAPTER TWENTY

BE CAREFUL WHAT YOU WISH FOR!

My goals for season 2012/13 were to catch more barbel, but not bigger. I would like to just catch and enjoy the pleasure. Finding a stretch of water where there are shoals of smaller fish to fulfil a desire to end a day's fishing with a smile on my face. ("What is confidence?". Paul Rogers, Barbel Fisher 34, Autumn 2012)

When I typed those words sometime in the close season 2012, the emotion was meant and heart-felt; I believed that to enjoy my limited fishing time, catching fish was more important than size. Well, eight months later, as autumn turned toward winter, I acknowledged that even though it had been achieved, all the while the addiction of the adrenaline rush of landing a big double was hard to withdraw from. Each capture had lifted my spirit, yet inside my thoughts were yearning for that next bite to be from the biggie.

The first week of the season was spent on the upper St Patrick's Stream, a beautiful piece of water meandering through the Thames Valley meadows in Charvil, Berkshire. As with most of England, it was buckling under the strain of that summer's floods, chocolate-brown and uninviting to the new member of the club controlling this waterway, but I was full of confidence, and expecting to catch sooner rather than later. The club members I had spoken to all said that the upper stretch was hard, populated to a lower level than downstream where St Pat's joins the River Loddon. They all said few fish came out in daylight, which just made me more determined to do well. However, apart from a reasonable eel within an hour on the first short trip and a couple of 4lb-plus chub later in the week, the feeling of failure crept in after just eighteen hours' fishing - far too soon, but patience is not a gift I have in abundance.

Despondent, with my tail between my legs, I retreated to a Thames weirpool for a day's fishing. I was greeted by what could only be described as a giant boiling pot of coloured fast-flowing water. However, after walking the short club stretch of seven swims, it became obvious that two areas could still be fished effectively, so the decision was made to try. After twenty minutes in the first-choice swim, being bothered by a feeling, a sixth sense of needing to move, I collected the tackle and strolled across a side-stream bridge to an area which gave some opportunity to ease the pressure of the season's first capture.

I found it easy to roll a 1oz flat lead into a slower piece of water on the edge of a deep, close-in channel. Baiting with a small piece of luncheon meat, the tip rattled after only five minutes, and my first barbel of the season was on. The fight was not prolonged, and in twenty seconds a fish of about 12oz slid into an oversized net! Buoyed by a fish, however, I soon had a bait back in the water. The tip was continually being moved, and half an hour later I landed a roach/bream hybrid of about half a pound; I believed these were the culprits causing the constant movement.

Changing over to a boilie, in this case a Wraysbury Baits 'Fifth Element' 14mm, and a stringer of four baits, I hoped that the hybrids would be less of a problem. By this time, it was 8.30pm, and as I had promised Marie, my wife, I would pack up at 9.00pm to get home at a reasonable time, the clock was ticking... Getting ready to pull the bait in, I stood next to the rod with all the other tackle dismantled - apart from the landing net, of course - when my mobile signalled a call from my wife - but I never got a chance to answer it, as the centrepin gave off its battle-cry.

Lifting into the fish, the realisation quickly hit home that this was a good one; solid and deep, the fish would not come off the bottom. In front of me were two large reed/bulrush beds, so I held the fish off in the current while I struggled into the waders that should have been on already. It behaved itself as I slid down into two feet of water where the swim should be, and slowly edged myself out to a position where netting would be possible. As the fish came over the net's rim, my arm was lifted in victory at the first decent fish of the season. At 11lb 13oz it was, unbeknown to me, the only double-figure barbel I would land over the summer/autumn period.

The next evening, it was impossible for me not to return; however, only the one bite materialised; at 7.20pm, a small judder on the rod-tip to a boilie fished on the crease. Striking on a hunch, the rod collapsed, being pulled round into a full loop by my adversary. Luckily, the waders were already on, and I slipped down into the water as the fish moved deep and fast downstream. This is where my luck started to change, as the fish moved downstream under the trailing branches of a big willow.

Under normal conditions, these branches would be three feet above the surface; today, they were struggling to keep out of the flow. One, larger than the rest, dipped deeper into the mucky layer below. The fish appeared to change direction; however, the only way I knew this was to watch the branch start to move across the current. The pressure was immense, and even though I could still feel the line moving it became harder. I believe the line had begun cutting into the wood and had become lodged, and as the pressure increased yet further, the size 10 hook pulled, and the end tackle flew past the branches and came free.

The stretch of water fished does regularly produce large carp; several could be seen in the mouth of the side-stream mentioned earlier, sheltering from the floodwater, with some in the low 30lb bracket - so could the lost fish have been one of these, or a big barbel? The fight lasted three minutes before the hook pulled, so I will never know.

With my tail once again firmly between my legs, the decision was made to move onto a new stretch of the River Loddon. This particular piece of water was approximately three hundred yards long, and being overgrown, there were only four recognisable swims; however, being careful to not make it look too obvious, I created five more in amongst the reeds and nettles. On my first visit, I met a club bailiff, who appeared to have very fixed views on the fishing. He told me that it was almost impossible to catch in daylight, and the numbers of fish were low. Well, being one to take a different path from others, I made it my challenge to try and catch a few. On that first trip I fished five different swims, more to find out the lie of the land than to catch.

For the lack of time one evening, a visit to the Lower St Pat's on a wet, miserable evening gave a capture. This stretch of water is a more heavily-fished section, and I ventured here just for a look before heading to the intended upper reaches for a short trip after work, but as the weather closed in, a decision was made to fish a likely-looking swim. It quickly produced a 6lb 9oz fish within five minutes of arriving. This fish only stands out as a first fish from the St Pat's, as it was caught more by luck than judgement; however, it got me off the starting block.

Returning to the Loddon for another four-hour trip, a decision was made to spend the same amount of time in the first clear swim on the stretch. The weather was hot and sunny, and the river had dropped nine inches from earlier in the month. A few loose baits were thrown lightly along the leading edge of the big willow; a 1oz lead and hookbait followed into what felt like about five feet of water against the branches. Every so often, the rod-tip would move slightly, suggesting interest from fish, but it was not until 8.25pm that the tip flew round.

Prior to this season, I had lost very few barbel (according to my records, only two in the previous five seasons), so when this fish went solid, I was not overly concerned, believing it would come free, but after fifteen minutes of coaxing, the realisation dawned that it was a lost battle. Any loss is painful, and the first fish from a new river was even more so.

Do you ever get the feeling that your luck may have changed? Eight more trips had taken place since, with only another lost fish to show for it. The fish had battled underneath a hawthorn bush for three minutes, and neither of us would give an inch, so when the fish came out into clear water I was gutted when the hook-length parted an inch up from the hook. Inspecting the line, it was almost destroyed: for over ten feet it was frayed - the worst state I had ever seen a line in. Even so, I believe there would have still been the strength to land the fish if given the chance, as I have full faith in the brand of line in use that season (Berkeley XTS 10lb).

My confidence had taken a battering, and I dearly needed to land a fish to get into the groove. So, another four-hour trip after work saw me settle into what I had called the Willow swim at 8.00pm, after spending some time in the Stump for a 43/4lb chub. The bait was swung into the deeper water along the margin, and fifty minutes later the tip moved slowly round. The strike met with little resistance; however, it did not feel like a chub, so a smile came to my face as a beautiful, small, perfectly-conditioned barbel slid over the net.

I chose to continue to fish the same stretch of the River Loddon for the next month, feeling that I was getting to grips with it. The challenge was still within my reach. Fishing conditions changed as the rivers became gin-clear and flowed at their normal summer levels, filling up with masses of weed, both streamer and cabbage, choking some swims to the point where finding a clear hole became difficult.

Having caught a barbel, my confidence felt on the up. Dropping into one of the smaller out-of-the way swims at 6.45pm on a warm, sticky evening, the bait was lowered over the reeds

by the undercut in six feet of water. Sitting back from the rods in the shade of a small tree, the waiting game began. Eight pm approached, and I was getting itchy feet, trying to decide 'should I stay, or should I go'? I collapsed the chair and stood back a little while, pondering, lost in thought - a screaming reel brought me back to the moment. The fight was not what I expected, and within a minute a large-looking barbel hit the net.

As I lay the barbel on the mat, it became obvious why she had performed so badly - she had the size of a 12/13lb fish, but her appearance was that of an old fish, with ragged fins; her colour was almost white/grey, and her belly was empty. I felt sorry for having caught her, as she looked like she was on her last fins. Weighing her quickly, I took one picture before I slid the 9lb 15oz fish back to her watery home.

Two weeks later, in the same swim, I decided to fish two rods, feeling that it was not too cramped; one rod was fished to the same position as last trip, and the other against the reeds on the right-hand side of the swim, with a bait cast along the margin towards the willow. I sat concentrating on the upstream rod, thinking that would be the one to respond first, which as we all know is bad angling - I awoke from a daydream as the 'pin on the other rod brought me back to reality. On lifting into the fish, it quickly dawned that it was a good one, but, while holding it hard to prevent it running into the roots below, something happened that left me sick. It had been many years since this had happened, so when the tackle came back without a hook-length and a curly-ended mainline, I knew the knot had slipped on the swivel. I test every knot I tie, so I had no reason why this occurred, and had to accept the loss, however bad I felt.

The summer water levels remained for the month of September, and I continued to plug away at the River Loddon stretch till the third week, when I felt it was time to return to the upper St Pat's, which had treated me badly on the first week of the season.

I didn't know what drew me to the chosen swim; every time I had looked at it earlier in the season, it felt as though my name was on it - hidden away from the swims either side, with a bank hardly trodden and a forest of nettles and other weeds to hide you from others walking past. Arriving at 4.00pm, I took fifteen minutes or so to check how the current moved and to guess the placement of any snags. There was a pronounced crease as the weed became less dense slightly downstream, which I felt would be the best bait position. I was able to use a four swan-shot link, helping me to create a slack line over the tail of the weed without dislodging the bait. Sitting back, hidden from view, all was right with the world as I watched the rod-tip for signs of life. Thirty minutes later, I was disturbed by a group of fighting swans coming through the narrow stretch of water in front of me. "That's my fishing gone for the day", I thought, but that lasted only a microsecond, as the rod-tip pulled round - not a massive fish, but it was my first from the upper St. Pat's, weighing 6lb 9oz. I was still pleased to have caught so quickly; however, no more followed that day.

October started as a month of high hopes, with me confidence at its peak and belief the fish will continue to come. It was a month of being unsettled, however, not sticking to any one stretch - and with an ever-decreasing number of hours to fish, I was up against it. As the evenings started to draw in, the time spent on the bank became more precious; not being one who enjoys after-dark fishing I normal pack up just into dark or at the most an hour after -So, apart from the Barbel society fish-in on the River Kennet's Lower Benyons at the beginning of the month no session lasted longer than three hours.

I had been asked by Pete Reading to support John Found and Phil Smith over the weekend of the Barbel Society's regional fish-in, as he was away fishing the Avon Project fundraiser. The two days past quickly, and it was not until afterwards that I realised that I only really fished no more than four hours each day. The only fish caught were on the Saturday, and I was fortunate to land one of 5lb or so off my second swim. I had been forced into a move by the rising river flooding my swim - foolishly, I was wearing short boots, not enough to stay put.

I decided to go to the top of the stretch, and while sorting myself out I dropped a bait fifteen feet out on a gentle crease. While I was still getting the tackle tidied, the rod-tip pulled round softly and a short fight saw me landing a beautiful small fish, which gave me hopes for more. Over another three hours, small knocks were shown on the rod-tip, but nothing worth striking, so I spent the rest of the day socialising.

Mid-month saw another quick fish from the upper St Pat's - I had only been fishing for an hour when an 8lb 2oz barbel gave the three foot-twitch we all love. Pleased with the capture, as the size was on the up, I was hoping for the doubles to appear. Several other fish came out throughout October, but nothing of real interest.

November is a time of year when personal bests have graced my net on two occasions, and I so wanted the same to be true this year. Well, only getting out for twelve hours over six trips in the first two weeks, my feet did not get near a river-bank afterwards. The nearest was on the 25th to look at the rising torrent that the River Loddon had become. If I had been feeling brave, a short stretch was fishable at lunchtime, but in hindsight the right decision was made, as the river continued to make a lake of the cornfields, flowing too powerfully to wade to safety.

So, no fish came my way all month, and at the time of writing in early December the hard frost on top of the high levels was not too promising for at least a few weeks - not for chub, either, as the water was so coloured.

So where has this left me?
The results are what I wished for, but I wanted more.

CHAPTER TWENTY-ONE

I CAME, I FISHED, AND I CAUGHT

After an enjoyable Summer and Autumn catching reasonable-sized small barbel from a couple of new rivers, I was in the same situation as most anglers throughout Britain, in that the rivers had become lakes of turbid, brown liquid that had no resemblance to fishable water. Even if it was fishable, I - and everyone else - was finding it difficult to get anywhere near it! There had been a short period in December when, if I had been brave enough in my neck of the woods, I could get down to the river - and a few did. I thought about it one Sunday afternoon after driving past a favourite stretch that was accessible, but when I went to look two hours later, I realised I would have been trapped on the raised bank with deep water behind me in the field, as the river had risen a couple of feet. Not wishing to become a statistic, a headline in a local paper, leaving a grieving wife, I turned tail and slunk back home to watch TV.

New Year's Day 2013 - I just had to get out and fish

Arriving at the car park next to the bridge crossing the bottom of the fishery, I walked over the bridge and stood looking downstream past the Waterworks pool. The footpath was only just passable, and knowing the swims, there may have been a couple to fish on that stretch; however, neither would be ones I would choose. The fishing bank of my chosen stretch was inaccessible along the path behind the cottages, so I stood and pondered on a plan of action: do I go home, or do I try and fish further upstream?

I was not in any rush, and when Joe and his dog came into view, I looked forward to a chat; I hadn't seen him all year, as I'd last fished here the previous season. Now Joe is a great old character, a countryman at heart; he would be as much at home with a rifle cocked over his arm on a shoot as he would with a split-cane rod and centrepin - an image not dissimilar to Jack Hargreaves doing the TV programme 'Out of Town' in the 1960's and '70s. His dog is another character in his own right; in the many years I have known Joe, it would always be the dog who would find me! Even if I was hidden away in a tight swim, he would come bounding – well, that is a slight exaggeration - as an old dog, he would wobble into the swim to greet me. He would sit next to me waiting for a few cubes of meat (the dog, not Joe), and Joe would usually appear a couple of minutes later.

When I fished here regularly from 2008 to 2011, I met Joe almost every trip I made. I believed he walked mile upon mile along this river from the large town downstream every day, along the river's main course and canalised stretches that interspersed it, all the way to the better-known barbel stretches most rushed to, bypassing these lower reaches, which do not have the same beauty or charisma, or the hallowed, hushed whispers of the giants caught upstream.

Each day, Joe would reminisce about the catches of yore, and the fishermen and country folk he had known through the years. I do not honestly know if Joe was his name - he never told me his name directly – but whoever he was, he appeared to have known many of the famous names of the distant past, and some not too distant; he would regale me with tales of companionship and friendships, and stories of those innocent days - which were not innocent, even to those who lived them. Today was no different; however, there was no joy in Joe's musing on the water before us. He told me he no longer spends time trying to catch what he believes to be too small a number of barbel; he had moved onto a large river not too far away, chasing the dreams flowing in its water. For once, I felt no encouragement in his tone, no enthusiasm, and an air of despair sounded through his voice. The glint in his eyes had frosted, no longer focused on what had been his beloved stretch of river.

Joe had lived on this river many years more than I, seeing it through all the changes the years brought to it: the straightening of its course, the creation of wide reed-beds as the slower inside of bends silted up, the years of plenty and the years of famine – years when weed choked the river, through the years when natural food suffered when it did not. I felt for Joe; I had moved on after only a few seasons, as the emotions were not the same - being younger, I strayed because of wishing for a change, but Joe had to go before he died with his dreams... If he had stayed, I feel he would have disappeared into the mist, becoming just a memory to those who knew him - just a ghostly figure seen from afar, to become a legend to tell the children about. Yet knowing Joe, he would find a home on the other river, rekindle his spirit and fish on; his dog would continue to wobble along the bank, finding others like me, and sit waiting for a morsel to be held out in a friendly hand.

As Joe wandered away to continue his journey, my parting words blew past him; he wanted to believe them, but his heart was not listening as I called: "I won't catch if I'm not fishing - a barbel is out there with my name on it". The words caught the breeze and silently lifted out of reach, travelling to where I did not have a clue; heard by whom, I do not know.

I picked up my tackle, and as though in a trance turned a hundred-and-eighty degrees and faced the wind; foot followed foot, and I walked along the canal section stretching for half a mile into the distance. Hope of finding a fishable swim was a long shot, faith in the unseen, drawn by a ribbon of belief. The walk soon became laboured; I was dressed for a day of low temperatures, and today had caught me out. When I left home, the cloud looked laden with moisture, and the temperature was only 4C. Somehow, the drive through town, my indecision, and talking with Joe had used three hours of fishing time - it was now almost midday, and the temperature had risen to a tropical 10C. Sweat, which my Wychwood, all-weather trousers which should allow to evaporate, plus my thick jumper, turned my face red and flushed. It seemed an eternity; the destination luring me on tricked me into thinking it was closer. I had never done this walk laden, and even the little tackle I had with me today, including the umbrella that came 'just in case', now felt like a ball and chain dragging at my heels.

Reaching the weirpool at the top of the stretch, the tackle was removed from my shoulders, and the chair dropped to the floor. Exhausted and overheating, wishing to collapse in a heap on the ground, I stood wiping my face with a tissue - a waste of time, as the sweat turned it to pulp. My breathing slowly returned to a more normal rate, my flushed face paled, and my body temperature became bearable - time to look around. Surprisingly, the realisation dawned that the water presented itself, accepting of the opportunity of a line being cast. The menace seen downstream and expected here was not present, only the somewhat steadier flow of deeper water the pool holds. Where my tackle lay, the top of the wall normally visible down to the swim was submerged, the top being lapped by the water, as the river was carrying four feet of extra depth.

I was faced with a dilemma; over the last season, the fishing bank of this stretch had changed. The local council had made a nature reserve on the bank on which I now stood, while the controlling angling association had been given the opposite bank, which was now completely underwater to a depth of a couple of feet. One small swim was available nearer the weir, but it wasn't fishable, as the water boiled into a 'witch's brew'. The swim below me marked the start of what had now become out of bounds, with overhead cables preventing safe fishing from that swim, so I needed to be made to stay where my tackle now lay.

Breaking rules has never figured in my methods; however, today I felt a risk had to be taken - if I was on a non-fishing bank and a challenge from a bailiff did come, I would put my hands up and move on. Not seeing a bailiff for many months, I didn't expect to see one today! While tackling up, one of the Brothers (a bit like the twins – if you know them) walked past with his wife. The Brothers cycle up and down the association's river, doing a great job, and he knew me well. Last season they had taken a picture for me of a double caught just before they had come upon me. Believing he would ask me to move on, a shock awaited me: he took no notice of where I was sat, and we chatted for ten minutes or more. He had been in hospital, and he had only just started to get out; as it was a nice day, he had chosen to walk along the canal with his wife. Bidding me farewell, he disappeared back from whence he had come.

Taking this as a good omen, I slowly put the rods together; one rod would be my preferred set-up, but today, to give myself a choice of baits and tackle placement, I had brought two along. The first rod was soon ready; with an 11/2oz flat pear lead, and a Wraysbury Baits 'Fifth Element' 12mm boilie covered in paste, the tackle was cast along a crease a rod-length out and twenty-feet downstream. The first bait entered the water at 12.45pm - only four hours after leaving home...

I as sat down to prepare the second rod, I was disturbed by a screaming Dave Swallow (centrepin) reel and a rod dancing in the rests. I picked up the rod, not striking; just a gentle lean into the rod with a finger stopping the spool had the desired effect. The rod took on a nice battle-curve; battle commenced, and a smiling angler embraced the pleasure and the warmth of the sun overhead. The fish didn't fight that hard; making several lunges into the main flow, it soon rose in the water close to the wall. How beautiful a barbel looks after a couple of months' glut, as the sun glinted on the bronzed, scaled flesh, her mouth opened as she slid into the waiting net.

It had been no more than five minutes, and a fish lay on the unhooking mat. Mesmerised, I allowed the pleasure to fill me. It was not a large fish; however, at 8lb 5oz I felt fulfilled and at peace with the world around me. Another cast was made, and again I slowly set up the second rod to be fished baited with a cube of luncheon meat further out on the edge of the main current pulling through the centre of the pool. Once this rod had been cast, I sat back and basked in the winter sun, pleased to be out, and believing I might be the only angler for some distance. Twenty minutes or so later, two Eastern European members of the association (I checked their tickets before they commenced fishing) set up to pike-fish behind me on the canal. We chatted about their last trip, when they had caught several pike to 19lb+ from where I was sat.

The two anglers returned to their swim, and I returned to my thoughts whilst watching the rod-tips gently knocking to the odd piece of flotsam bouncing around in the current. Time passed slowly; the kingfisher flew past onto the flooded field below the pool. What should be a landscaped nature reserve was covered with over a foot of water; the man-made lagoons were all joined as one, and judging by the number of fish-eating birds, many small fish had taken up residence out of the force of the current in their usual home.

While watching the activity of the birds, out of the corner of my eye a movement on the rod fishing meat drew my attention back. A couple of sharp knocks followed in the next few seconds before the tip slowly pulled round two feet. Striking this fish, it felt more powerful than the last, and on getting into the main flow it made a strong run downstream. As it slowed and turned back towards me, I realised that it was only thirty minutes since landing the earlier fish. I wondered if the day was going to be magical, a winter's day blessed - what more could I ask for?

As the fish approached the landing net, it was clearly large enough to be a double. Once more, the bronze beauty shone a vision of illumination personified. Letting it rest in the net, I prepared my camera for a self-take, and ensured all was ready to bring her ashore. On weighing, the digital scales held at 10lb 5oz; photographs were taken, and the fish was held in the water until she kicked strongly away.

Expectantly and overly confident, I swung a bait back to the same spot, yet 1.00pm became 4.00pm and no more bites came my way. The rod fishing the boilie had been forgotten; rebaiting with a fresh bait, it was swung further along the crease. Time ticked slowly, and my thoughts drifted to the recent memory - how might my chances of catching more be improved? All questions were answered; I was already doing enough, and my confidence kept me from changing anything in my set-ups or moving the position of the baits – a sixth sense whispered in my subconscious, and I stayed put. The sunlight became a filtered glow through the trees of the western bank opposite, moved by an unseen hand toward the horizon, bringing the dawn of the moon rising behind me in the east – the creation of a whimsical, scented stage, set for the final act of the day. Sitting there, I waited for the climax of the show.

The sun touched the horizon with its leading edge as the meat rod lurched tip-first towards the water's surface, and a centrepin's scream, banshee-like, cut through the emotional silence that had preceded it. The robin that was sitting under the rod fled in horror. This fish stayed deep; connected to the gravel as though part of it, it glided gracefully, full of power. Could this be the hoped-for giant? Deep down I knew it was good - however, not that great. Slowly she rose to the surface, lying there in perfection; my net opened to let her rest in the mesh, and a low-double flared her fins in defiance. Allowing her to rest, the routine was again followed: set up camera, weigh, photograph, and rest again; 11lb 0oz she gave me, to record in my fishing log; a pleasing result at the end of the day.

I hardly noticed that the temperature had fallen out of the day; the expected cloud cover did not arrive to keep the warmth in, and the frost started to grip the wet net and chill my fingers. Home beckoned: the call of a warm bath and a celebratory glass of wine was a stronger pull upon the soul than catching another barbel. If hope still played its magical tune, another might come my way, but having used up my brownie points, and having told my wife I would be home by 6.00pm, it was time to go.

Was it that it was cooler, was it that the flask was empty, or was it that a weight had lifted off my soul? The walk along the towpath had an enriched, quickened pace compared to the one on arrival; no sweating, but my glow of triumph lit the way into the moon's glow glinting off the frosty path.

The drive, which would normally get me frustrated, stuck in slow moving traffic on the A33 into town, passed free of anger at the other drivers; I had no need to rush - the journey was already complete.

CHAPTER TWENTY-TWO

CASTER AT CASTOR

As in the previous year, the last two days of the season were spent fishing with my brother Jeff. For a second year, we returned to a water of our younger years; during the early 1980s we would regularly fish Castor Backwater on the River Nene, just outside Peterborough in Cambridgeshire. During the intervening years, our fishing paths took different directions; I had moved down South and became obsessed with fishing for large carp in the Colne Valley, while Jeff, for his sins, involved himself in match fishing, and spent far too much time (or at least that is what I jokingly told him) sitting with fourteen metres of roach pole and no.16 power elastic trying to fill as many keepnets as he could in four/five hours on a carp puddle! In 2007, my love for carp diminished, and I found myself a new lover - barbel! Moving onto the local rivers near Reading, excitement returned, realising the dream that had been there since my childhood, when seeing my first barbel on holiday in Christchurch fishing the Throop fishery on the Dorset Stour.

The annual fishing trips had started several years before, when Jeff treated me to two days on the Royalty Fishery on the Hampshire Avon, fishing the Compound Pool, for my fiftieth birthday. Until that time, we had been unlucky not to find the time to fish together since our youth. We would meet up a few times a year; however, as we aged, life commitments ate into our time. Every year we would insist we would get out at least once each season, but it never materialised. That first trip took place in June 2008, and we managed another two years before yet again work and family life got in the way! However, we had great times in Christchurch, as much the drinking in the evening as the fishing; we didn't take the river apart, yet it was fun trying to catch a barbel or two.

During the two years we were unable to get a trip together, we would talk about the possibility of trying nearer to home, and Castor Backwater came to our attention. I had read a couple of articles in 'Barbel Fisher' written by Mark Smith, the bailiff for Peterborough and District Angling Association on the backwater, and one by Barry Fisher, which fired my imagination. Odd reports of doubles came through in the angling press, too, and talking to John Newman (another B.S. member from Peterborough) at a Berkshire regional meeting was all it needed to plant the seed and put a plan into action.

In 2013, I regularly visited my mother, who lives near Jeff in Whittlesey, just outside Peterborough. Four times that year I travelled up with my wife for family get-togethers or to see her if she was unwell. The Backwater is only five or six miles away, and when I told Jeff about the barbel that were being caught, we were both determined to make a concerted effort to arrange a trip before the end of the season in March 2014. Little did we know how close to the end of the season it would be - we eventually set the dates for March 13th and 14th, which was cutting it fine! It was agreed that I would stay at Jeff's, and in the evening visit mum.

A little history

The Backwater is a beautiful little stretch of water, flowing for approximately ¾ mile through farmland close to the A1, the noise of cars and lorries constantly in the background. It has changed plenty through the years; the bends appear to have smoothed out, and a large bay used to be where what is now known as the Gate swim. We used to fish the bay for pike in February and March as they came into the Backwater to spawn in large numbers; catching gudgeon (do not see many of them nowadays), we would trot them under a two-swan loafer and catch as many as ten pike in an afternoon. Never did we get a 10lb fish; the best, at 9lb 15oz, showed our honesty.

What had drawn our attention to the Backwater in the first place was the reported capture of a 12lb barbel - front page news in the Angling Times in 1969! However, we never landed a barbel over the six years we fished there, but on several occasions we hooked and lost very powerful fish, all when using a light leger (3 or 4 swan-shot links) against the bank with luncheon meat or cheese as bait. In those days, a heavy line for me would be 6lb breaking strain, and on most occasions, I would be tackled up with less (4lb). It would be many years until a barbel would grace my net on the Backwater; we were content catching mid-sized chub on floating crust, legered meat/cheese, or trotted maggot alongside the dace, roach and gudgeon.

The first trip to the Backwater in thirty years

During the preceding years, I never really thought much of the Backwater; gravel pits in the Colne Valley were my fishing haunts, mainly creeping up on margin-feeding carp with light float tactics. I gained a couple of nicknames for my trouble; one is still in use today, and in a strange way I have become accustomed to it - and even feel proud of it.

From the time we formulated the plan for the end of the season, everything moved swiftly; our excitement grew, and tackle was made ready. Even though I didn't need to re-spool my reels, I did it anyway; new hooklengths were tied, and no knot was left untested. My relaxed approach to a fishing trip disappeared, and I felt like a little kid before their first flight on a plane, going on holiday and not wanting to forget a thing.

It had been decided that I would meet Jeff at the car-park on the Backwater on the 13th March, leaving home in Reading for a two-and-a-half hour journey; I intended to arrive by 10.30am. There was only one other car when I arrived, but Jeff was running late; it was really difficult to wait for him, and I kept looking up the track, willing him to get there sooner. Just before 11.00am, Jeff pulled up alongside me; pleasantries exchanged, we soon had our tackle upon our backs to walk the 200 yards to the bridge over the Backwater. Standing on the bridge gazing upstream, old memories came flooding back.

The decision was made to stay on the north bank, and we set the tackle down where the river bends up to the Gate swim. The swim in front of us, in 1984/5, produced some of our best trips, but now it had changed; we used to trot down to what in those days was a very shallow, weedy riffle (less than a foot deep), but now the shallows are three times deeper, and a swim called the Barbel Tree resides there. On the bend itself, the spot is named the Nursery, due to the snaggy, far-bank bay created as a fish refuge.

Jeff chose to start in the Nursery, and I felt it a good idea to try in the Barbel Tree, so we spent a couple of hours there before Mark Smith, the bailiff, came on his rounds. He appeared to be knowledgeable, and his tips were taken on board. One tip, though, was not really what we had wanted to hear. We had come prepared to fish maggot/caster over hemp, but Mark said this didn't work well there... If you know me well, that was a 'red rag to a bull' - if someone tells me something will not work, I will go out of my way to prove them wrong. We had brought with us approximately 10lb of hemp and six pints of maggots and caster to last the two days; for back-up we had luncheon meat and my favourite mini-boilies.

Pellets do not play a part in my fishing, and had not since 2007, when after much soul-searching I stopped using them due to a belief founded on writings by more knowledgeable anglers than me, stating that the overuse of pellets is harmful, due to the excessive amounts of oils in them being dangerous, either because of becoming rancid or, in the case of oils used in fish-farming, because of the de-sexing of fish. To make farming profitable, fish need to gain weight, not use up energy spawning and creating eggs. However, this is a digression, and really needs to be addressed in another forum. I do wish this would happen; if we wish our sport to continue, we have to become more responsible for the fish we chase, and the 'catching the largest at any cost' mentality needs to be curtailed. We all want to beat PB's, but is it worth it in the long run?

Anyway, after sitting in the first swims for a couple of hours, trying to build the swims up slowly, nothing was happening, so the decision was made to move upstream. We didn't go far; I chose the Gate swim and dropped some bait into the deeper margin before going for a walk up to the weirpool for inspiration. Everything had changed - it was impossible to remember what it had looked like thirty years ago in the long-lost past.

Jeff began fishing slightly upstream, and I believe his match-fishing attitude started to kick in, as he became happy snatching the silvers on swimfeedered maggot. My approach was to sit it out with both baits dropped into five feet of water under the rod-tip: meat upstream and caster another ten feet downstream. Apart from a couple of half-pulls on the meat, I ended the day without even a silver to my name.

Packing up at 6.00pm, we left the inquest until we got back to Jeff's home. His wife Denise was very patient with us; over dinner all we talked about was how we could improve on the day's results. We compromised on a plan, agreeing to fish close to Jeff's second swim, so after a bottle of wine (or two) we staggered off to our respective beds with the idea of rising at 6.30 in the morning.

On waking, we were greeted to different weather to the previous day, when the sun has shone brightly and only a slight breeze had ruffled the water; today had broken with thick cloud cover and a chill in the air. It felt several degrees lower in temperature, and we both needed an extra layer of clothing.

However, by 7.00am we were heading out of the door, eager for a good day, but something was not right - which we didn't find out until we arrived at the swims! In our haste to get to the river, we had forgotten to take the maggots and caster out of the fridge - this meant a drive home for Jeff. We had travelled in his car, and he had to fight the rush-hour traffic; his mood had not been that bright, to say the least, but he took it well, and even stopped to get bacon rolls for breakfast.

While he was gone, I bravely fished on with meat in the chosen swim; however, I just didn't feel comfortable, and after eating my roll I suggested to Jeff that I took a wander to get a feel of other swims that might work for the 'social' style of fishing. So off I went with a rod, net, and a handful of bait - and the scales in my pocket just in case! My first stop was in the tail of the weirpool, where I spent twenty minutes before moving down to the swim now called Weedy Corner. The swim itself didn't feel right, but the area below, which would have been in a big reed-bed in summer, looked much better. After casting around to get a feel of the swim, I moved on again, with the intention of suggesting to Jeff that we should move there later if we hadn't had any joy.

On the way back to Jeff, a sixth sense drew me into a tight little swim, requiring a scramble through undergrowth to present a bait under an overhanging bush. There was only room to gently swing the bait underarm, so I used a small swimfeeder to rest the bait and three-bait stringer on top of a tiny plug of groundbait to prevent the long hook-length from snagging on the trailing branches. The bait had only been in place for a minute or so when the tip slammed round; how I missed it, I don't know, but it happened. Quickly, another bait was swung into the swim. On this occasion there was a wait of three minutes, and again the rod buckled, and I was connected to a very lively fish.

After a short fight, a barbel of just over 6lb lay in the folds of the landing net. My spirits were lifted by this result; however,

I was aware this trip was meant to be a social with my brother, so I returned to Jeff with the news of the capture and began encouraging him to move to the swim below Weedy Corner. I hadn't noticed another angler walking past, and when I took Jeff up to look at the swims, dismay came over me - the other angler had beaten us to it. Little did we know at the time that he would move, and we found ourselves setting up there only a couple of hours later.

I would like to write that we took the swims apart; however, my swim under the tree only produced a pike of about 8lb that took a piece of meat on the retrieve - crashing around in the swim, it scared everything that swam for yards up and downstream. This may have helped Jeff, but both fish he hooked were lost quickly: one to a hook-pull and the other a slipped knot.

We packed up at 6.00pm, knowing we could/should have done better, yet realising that it was now past, and if we could learn from the lessons of the two days, then next year would achieve more. During the day, we had already agreed to make the same trip next year, when we would make amends.

March 12th and 13th 2015 - The Return Match

Season 2014/15 had been good to me, catching well from a new stretch of the River Loddon; using a particle approach on daylight visits, I felt positive about the return trip to Castor Backwater with Jeff. On the previous trip, we had been convinced that a similar style of fishing would work, even though we had been told otherwise. The lessons learnt during the summer and autumn on the Loddon increased my confidence, and made me more determined to succeed at catching some barbel from the Backwater in March on caster.

However misled our plan was, we still had faith in an approach which would appear to catch well on similar waters; while most anglers set their stall out to catch the larger fish with pellets, meat, and boilies, the Backwater should respond in a positive way to the caster and hemp approach. After the previous year's lack of barbel, it would have been easier to join the crowd from the off, but my stubborn nature made me stick to the plan – just to prove everyone else wrong! Again, I took 10lb of hemp, and this time six pints of caster. The weather forecast for both days encouraged this approach, saying it would be overcast but warm for the time of year,

To give us more time fishing, I had travelled up to Peterborough the night before, and after a restful sleep we awoke to a perfect 'angler's dawn' - a slightly overcast sky, with the promise of a light breeze blowing downstream and a hint of some sun to warm us later in the afternoon. This year, the drive down Station Road seemed longer, not getting to our destination quick enough.

Unloading the car, the apprehension could almost be felt physically, a presence of excitement, an unheard scream in the air; words unspoken drew us across the railway tracks and onto the banks, where we were greeted with the sight of a river flowing in beautiful harmony within its banks, carrying a slight tinge of colour, with silver-fish topping, teasing us; knowing that their bigger brethren lay in wait, our steps became purposeful towards the chosen swims, decided over a glass of wine the evening before.

Instead of sticking to the northern bank as everyone else appears to do, the choice had been made to climb over into the gated field of the opposite bank. Walking three hundred yards, we put the tackle gently down behind a swim that the locals call Redmire. An instinct, a sixth sense had drawn me here, and feeding the swim with hemp and caster with a bait-dropper gave me a surprise; in mid-river I found a deep hole over ten feet deep – the fast water was diverted towards my bank, and the hole lay on the crease, the water becoming shallow towards the tree across the river. This hole ran for about six feet before sloping upwards to a depth of six feet.

Twenty-five yards downstream, Jeff's swim could not have been more different; nowhere in his swim could he find more than four feet of water, and the pace increased as the width of river had narrowed by a third. We baited up and went for a wander to let the swims settle. Well, I would like to say that one of us took the Backwater apart from these swims, but nothing was further from the truth, and after four hours of plugging away at feeding and waiting, it was Jeff who made the break first.

His new swim was opposite where he had lost two fish on the last day in 2014; I believe he thought he would have a good chance of a fish, and only ten minutes later an old chap who had walked past me a couple minutes before ran back and asked me to bring my scales - Jeff had a barbel on the bank! His bait had only been in the water for a short while, and he had only just got himself comfortable when the rod-tip flew round. A hard fight followed, with him landing a fish of 7lb 12oz. However, we had a dilemma - it had come to meat, not the expected caster. Did we give up on the plan, or turn our heads into the wind and keep on trying to succeed?

I continued to fish Redmire for another hour and a half without even the smallest of movements to the rod. For another hour I trotted single caster through the swim without a touch; my patience drifted away, and with my tail between my legs I moved up nearer to Jeff, and fished meat on two rods into a five-foot-deep glide. All we caught for the rest of the day were small chub to 1lb or so; on packing up, however, we weren't as despondent as the last time, as a barbel had been landed and we still had another day.

As with the previous year, an evening of navel-gazing while eating and drinking seemed to be quickly followed by the dawning of the second day. This year, it appeared as though God/the gods were against us more severely; the journey from hell awaited us. We had not really got ourselves moving until 8.00am, and this meant trying to get across Peterborough from Whittlesey in the middle of the rush-hour. Every road Jeff tried was solid with single-occupant cars or loaded people carriers with two kids and a yuppie mum - all trying to get nowhere fast! Jeff, normally patient and calm, became a banshee, foaming at the mouth; I wasn't really helping, as trying to talk calmly just seemed to make it worse. The journey that should have taken twenty minutes lasted over an hour, and we were glad to get out of the car. However, it was not over yet; I was about to receive my comeuppance - and it really hurt!

Having sat in the car for a long time, I hadn't thought about a stretch or two when I got out; so, when my back twinged as I pulled my bag onto my shoulder, it should have been taken as a warning. Reaching the gate to climb over, I lowered the tackle slowly over, but the bait-box of hemp required a longer stretch, and I doubled over in pain as I tried to step over with it and turned my back - locking into a spasm, it gave way. Now, being on the riverbank side of the gate I would have to try and climb back if I wanted to go back home, but nothing was further from my mind; tears were running down my face, but I wasn't going to give up. The pain was intense, and I bent double, letting out a terrifying scream - the dead of the churchyard across the field would have been scared! There was no way I would give in; knowing it would ease gave me the courage to fight on.

Jeff decided the best course of action would be for him to walk up to the chosen swims with his tackle, and then return for mine, while I walked slowly behind. As he walked away, I began to do some stretching exercises, making sure I didn't lie in a cow-pat in the process. All I could think of was that it was going to be a wasted day; however, over the fifteen minutes it took for Jeff to return, the pain eased, and movement became less troublesome. It was possible for me to lift my rods and chair, and walking at a snail's pace I covered twenty yards(!) by the time Jeff got to me. It was another twenty minutes before we had covered the three hundred yards to the swims - all I had to do now was set up and try to fish!

Dropping in about thirty yards upstream of Jeff, who had gone straight to the swim he caught the barbel from yesterday, I found a flat bank in amongst the dead reeds, which allowed a reasonably comfortable sitting position. Everything was placed close by, and I began tackling up. My first cast was at 9.55am: a small cube of meat was swung a couple of rod-lengths downstream on a four-foot tail with six swan-shot as weight. Straight away, the rod-tip was flicking to movements in the swim, and within five minutes I was playing a spirited 7lb 8oz barbel.

My back took the strain, making me feel much better, and I settled into the fishing, setting up a float rod with caster off the rod-tip. To give this rod a chance, the bait-dropper was used to put a bed of a couple of pounds of caster and hemp down – what fish could resist this? Well, apart from the occasional small roach or dace, it seemed the chub and barbel could. All day the bait

was constantly topped up, being placed just off the bank into seven foot of steady-paced water. Knowing the barbel were not too far away, having caught one already, it appeared a certainty that the crow-quill would go under at least the once, and I would find myself attached to a barbel.

While waiting for action, my thoughts mulled over the reasons for caster not seeming to work here - two trips and two anglers fishing should have given some result. Talking to locals before, there had been no positive feedback, yet on the day before a float angler had caught a barbel of eight pounds on single trotted caster - the same angler sat by the bridge, and had lost another. It was not that barbel did not like the caster; it was they just did not appear to want them stationary over a big bed of hemp. Every other small river where I have used this technique has produced both summer and end of season... More questions than answers, and none I felt able to find one to.

I spent a while talking it over with Jeff, and we came to the same conclusion - the following year, our trip would not be with hemp and caster - yet a nagging thought would stay with me all year, and no doubt I would still bring them along just in case! Returning to my swim feeling a little more comfortable due to the walking, I continued to do gentle exercises to keep the back pain under control, but as the day wore on, the need to get up and pace slowly behind the swim became more of a need. When Jeff suggested packing up early, I felt relieved, but frustrated for him, too: all he had caught had been a few small chub, which would have been alright if I didn't go and catch another!

Still fishing at 4.20pm; the float rod had been abandoned, and a piece of meat was being fished along the bank twenty feet downstream.

No knocks preceded the rod-tip slamming round, and I picked up the rod before the centrepin screeched. A heavy fish bore away as I leant forward slowly to prevent putting my

now-cold back into spasm. Lowering myself to a kneeling position in the reeds, straightening my back and letting the rod control the fish, there was no need to panic. Jeff quickly came over, and again started snapping away with the camera.

Twenty minutes later, a friend, John Newman, arrived, and as we were leaving soon, planning to pack up before 5.00pm, I agreed to him dropping into his favourite swim opposite and just below me. Packing away was not as painful as expected, and I was able to carry my own tackle back to the car. We stopped on the bridge as we crossed the Backwater, looking upstream and bidding farewell for another season, with hopes to return during the summer to be considered - breathing in the scenery, we said good-bye to Castor for now.

CHAPTER TWENTY-THREE

2014 - GETTING MY MOJO BACK

While waiting with apprehension for tomorrow to come, feeling faith in good fortune, hoping a better season than the last lay ahead - for tomorrow was the sixteenth of June - a new river season beckoned me, and whispered its spell of intoxication as of old. Having not cast a line for the twelve weeks of the close season, memories returned of the years long past, of how the excitement drew me in - the burning desire within me kept me awake; like a young child, I dreamt of what I believed would come – however, would it meet my expectations?

Barbel had become the fish that excited me the most; plans were made through the twelve-week sabbatical as to where and how I would fish – and were now coming to fruition. A local Thames weirpool cried out for my attention, and one swim in particular had my name on it. The day dawned bright and still, and with dew-soaked grass brushing on my trouser-covered ankles I widened my stride, hurrying to the chosen spot. Having arrived at first light, only one other angler was present, who also had a chosen swim - thankfully not mine.

Standing on the high bank behind the swim, I breathed in the mystical atmosphere, breathing in the pulse of the life-blood of my surroundings. A gentle mist rose off the river's mirrored surface, not giving away the secrets of the deep, flowing water below. Lowering myself slowly and safely down the steep bank, a small rodent, scared by my movement, scurried away. The swim enabled a seat to be positioned behind the high reeds twelve feet out in the water, on a small gravel patch at the base of the slope; the rod would be placed on rests in a foot of water, its tip only just protruding through the reeds.

No rush, just a quiet, hushed setting-up of tackle. I had prebaited the swim the night before, therefore there was no need for more than the first cast, touching the surface with hardly a sound to signal my presence, as the 1oz flat lead dropped through the surface to touch down in the deep run one-and-a-half rods out. The waiting game began; mesmerised by the gentle swaying of the reeds, dreams held my thoughts for two hours before the centrepin reel became a spinning blur.

As the rod buckled over, there was no doubt it was a big fish; however, something wasn't right - after keeping the fish out of the sunken tree a couple of times, it proceeded to fight just below the surface, chasing about at great speed. The first time it boiled close enough for identification confirmed my doubts, as a common carp looking about 20lb shot away once more. Landing this fish gave a flutter of the heart, but surprisingly the emotion was staid and reserved, and struggling to take a few pictures and weighing it at 21lb 2oz in the tight swim without pulling it up the bank produced only half-usable pictures. On being returned, the carp kicked its tail, soaking me as it tore off through the rushes.

Anguish was not the emotion expected; I had been waiting for the first fish of the season, and when it arrived I felt empty - the feeling of hunger half an hour after eating a Chinese meal, the come-down off a euphoric high... Was it going to be harder than I thought to shift the low of last year? 2013 had been my worst season's fishing for barbel, landing only a handful, and all 5-7lb. I had caught chub up to 6lb 1oz, a personal best, but they didn't light the fire, either. What did I need to get my mojo back?

A distraction gave me the opportunity not to think too much of my own feelings. As the Regional Organiser for Berkshire for the Barbel Society, I had a couple of fish-ins to set up for the beginning of July. Getting anglers to come, getting information to them, and liaising with the club who were allowing us to use their stretches of river all kept me busy, and I only got out fishing for a couple of short sessions on the pool with nothing to show.

The weekend of the fish-ins arrived; I had not been on either of the two stretches of river to be fished to even check on swim conditions, so I was way off the grapevine when it came to helping the anglers attending. In hindsight, I hope that no one felt hard done by; I learnt the lesson and intended being more proactive for future fish-ins on the same stretches. Over the two days, only three barbel were hooked; I fluked out a double on the Sunday from the River Loddon, from a stretch I had only fished once eight years ago for an afternoon.

This fish was the kick up the bottom needed to get me to try harder; the stretch of river awakened in me an exploratory spirit. It may be a piece of water that does see the presence of too many anglers at times, being only fishable for about five hundred metres; however, this season - from what I saw - it was being lightly fished (well, that was before a 15lb fish was meant to have come out in early September!). Fishing an afternoon session on Sunday each week and a short evening before the nights drew in, I was able to get to know the swims and methods to fish.

Over the month of July, I experimented with various methods, and fished a third of the swims. At a conservative guesstimate, there are thirty swims to be fished, but many seem to be barren shallows, at summer water levels no more twelve inches deep, with no weed, and in deep shadow all day due to the tunnel of trees. Fish may move through these swims, but I have yet to see any barbel in them, and little evidence of silver-fish, too. Along the length there are two islands, and the shallow swims are alongside them: the deeper channel runs on the opposite side of the island, making it unfishable. Overall, the stretch is nearly seven hundred metres long, but an out-of-bounds area a third of the way along takes away approximately over a hundred metres.

To complicate matters: as we know, barbel can be nomadic, travelling some distance if the mood takes them, and this piece of water is only part of over two miles of river, with no obstacles preventing their travel. I believe that some days the majority of fish may be in residence elsewhere.

Those first weeks only produced one small barbel in a rather overgrown, weedy swim, fishing hemp and caster for the first time. This fish came in the middle of a warm, sticky afternoon with small perch and chub pestering me, encouraging me to not follow this baiting path and keep plugging away with small boilies. Foolishly, I fell for my own delusion, and caught no more barbel until August Bank Holiday Monday, when, knowing I had a full day, I had purchased a couple of pints of caster and packed six pounds of hemp, intending to 'bait and wait'.

I fished a swim at the bottom of the fishery that allowed an angler to be undisturbed downstream, as the undergrowth was so bad that no one could get to the river for thirty yards below the swim. Beds of weed waved in unison with the steady flow over four feet of clear water, passing over beautiful clean gravel. A high bank opposite gave security from intrusion, and above there was no sign of the swim being fished from there. Baiting consisted of thirty small droppers of hemp and caster on the edge of the trailing willow branches in mid-river, which, as it was narrow, meant swinging the dropper no more than ten feet out. The weed cover between me and the baited position would give confidence to both me and the fish; if I stayed low and quiet, the barbel would feed confidently along its edge.

The swim was made ready, and I put the rod onto low rests, only having a foot of rod showing past the river's edge in a small gap in the bank-side plant growth. I chose a free-running flat 1oz lead; a feeder might have been a good option, but I felt more confident to feed by dropper with the tackle in the water. Every half an hour, I dropped three or four more droppers just short of the lead.

I had arrived at 8.00am, and after preparing the swim I had walked around upstream or talked to a couple of carp anglers further down on the lake behind me. Patience is not my best virtue; trying not fish for two hours is painful, but knowing it will produce the results makes it all worthwhile. 10.00am came, and I quietly crept back into the swim; four casters were super-glued onto a braided hair and the tackle was swung gently out, entering the water with no more disturbance than a small pebble. This was followed with three droppers of feed before I sat down in my chair, a rod-length back from the water's edge.

Only ten minutes later, the Dave Swallow centrepin screeched, and the rod-tip was bouncing; on striking, the fish knew where it wanted to be – however, showing it who was boss, I soon had it resting in the net. The rain that had been falling all morning, and that would continue for the rest of the day, didn't dampen my mood; the fish had broken the spell of melancholy, peace comforted the soul - this was what I had been waiting for. Little did I know at the time that this was the beginning of a time of plenty...

Twice more that day the reel signalled to me that a fish had been hooked; they ranged between five and eight and a quarter pounds, and one of these fish took the bait as I was lowering the third dropper of bait over it! I packed up earlier than planned, as I had used all the bait by 4.00pm; also, my spirit had lifted, and I didn't want to break the spell.

In the next four weeks, I fished a further six trips, one a short evening with a larger bait, catching nothing; however, with hemp and caster I hooked two barbel every trip, the largest being a 12lb 2oz fish - my best for over three years. All the fish were coming in the middle of the day, from 10.15am to 6.00pm; I didn't know if my captures would improve if I fished into the dark - most of the other anglers were fishing later, but I wondered if their catch rate was any better?

Where do I go from here? Do I continue just fishing the one stretch using the hemp and caster approach for the rest of the season, or at least until the winter brings us the high, coloured water that calls for large smelly baits - or do I spread myself thinly and chase fish here, there, and everywhere? In my normal routine, I am only able to get out fishing for six to eight hours during the day at the weekend, wishing that wasn't so and wanting to fish more often; yet do I go fishing as a competition, or is it for enjoyment...?

These thoughts are a constant within my life, not just angling - do we always want bigger and better? Have we forgotten the pleasure of enjoyment, lost the innocence of childhood, bought into the dream of false hopes, believing that we can achieve more and then paying the price for our delusions? If, by acknowledging this constant quest to be the best, we have the ability to raise ourselves above it, to separate the dream from reality and know the difference - we are free to enjoy again. The 2014/15 season re-lit my innocence, enabling me to taste joy and pleasure from my fishing - may we all be able to continue to enjoy fishing, too.

CHAPTER TWENTY -FOUR

ARE BARBEL PSYCHIC?
OR
HOW DO THEY KNOW WE HAVE
TAKEN OUR EYE OFF THE ACTION?

I ask that you bear with me for a moment while I explain the title: I do not for a moment believe that any fish - including barbel - can read our minds, nor do they have magical powers; if they did, I honestly believe we would never catch them at all, as they would know every bait with a hook attached, and where it is! There are times, however, when we may feel this as we finish the session without a bite or sign of fish in the swim!

So, what am I alluding to? It is those moments when we take our eye off the rod-tip and a bite occurs, pulling the rod off the rests if the clutch is not set correctly or the free-spool is not engaged; for those of us using centrepin reels, the spool goes into overdrive as the barbel powers away downstream.

This happens more often than most of us would acknowledge, and some occasions are laughable; however, a positive outcome still prevails. Others bring about rage, as we see the rod being dragged through the water's surface.

Before fishing seriously for barbel, I spent many years on the gravel pits of the Colne Valley, angling for carp - and how often did a take come while relieving myself in the bushes, or boiling a cup of tea on a small stove...? One particular situation comes to mind: not on a Colne Valley pit, but a small Cambridgeshire lake in the depths of winter. To fish the swim in question, it was only possible to get a bait in the correct position by wading out to the edge of the reeds and gently casting underarm along their edge to a small bush. The rod(s) (normally, one would go along the reeds and another would be fished to open water), would be placed on tall rests in the water, allowing for the tip of the reed rod to be far enough out to be past the leading edge of the reeds.

The swim had a very high back behind it, and not wanting to be far from the rods to prevent a snagged carp in the reeds, I would place my seat just behind the rods – and, at that time of year, get cold feet in my waders. Every so often, I would stand up and move back onto a small, dry patch of gravel; at about three in the afternoon one day, I had done so, and as I stood with unzipped winter clothing and my manhood out, the reed rod tore off, with the buzzer (which was turned up too loud) screaming, alerting me to action. Turning to face the rod, I am still unsure of what happened; the rod had been dragged forward, the reel appeared lodged in the buzzer - and the rod -rest was being pulled out of the ground, too! I managed to stop the rod and rest going out into the lake, untangled the rod-tip from the extremities of the reeds, and began playing the carp. Well, I would love to say I landed a beast of thirty-pounds-plus, but alas - it was a fish of just over 10lb.

We would all like to believe that each mistake will enable us to learn and grow; however, I still have this happen, as no doubt each of us also suffer from the consequences of taking our eye off the action. When I first started fishing for barbel again in 2007, I used a fixed-spool reel for the majority of my fishing, and after a few trips of missed takes when using a Baitrunner, the decision was taken to fish with a tighter clutch setting on the reel instead. The bites being received were not the usual three-foot twitches, which seemed to be the reason for not setting the hook; my mind-set was to strike and set the free-spool in one action, but the shorter takes meant that I was not resetting the spool on the strike – however, this then created problems of its own.

During the following two seasons, the numbers of barbel on the stretches of the River Kennet I fished meant that on more occasions than not, a take would come within minutes of the first cast. Now, how many of us only fish the one rod, or have everything set up before that first cast? Unless we are fishing a particle approach, baiting with bait-droppers, our bait is placed quickly if we only have a limited time to fish. So, on a regular basis I would be messing around in my tackle, setting up my chair, and moving tackle about so it was within easy reach, when the movement of the rod dragging over the bank, or being hit in the leg as it swung round, would bring me back to the action. If we all had a pound for each time this has occurred, some of us would be rich men, but nowadays it appears to happen less on the stretches fished.

For all the right reasons, I remember one occasion, if only for the capture of a previous personal best caught in November 2009. Arriving at a swim that I had looked at many a time but never fished, I loose-fed some hemp and luncheon meat before deciding to start elsewhere for an hour or two to let the swim settle. The river had been over its banks for the previous two weeks, and to get to the sitting position I had to squish through sticky reed-beds when I came back to this swim. I sat on a slightly raised area of bank to take in the river in front of me. There was a steady flow of water down to the willow thirty feet downstream, so the decision was made to cast the ready-baited tackle level with the outside of the branches. Resting the rod on the bank while I sorted out the right rod-rests, I was taken aback as the butt of the rod crashed into my thigh, followed by the forward movement of the rod and the tip sinking into the bank-high water before I managed to grasp the reel-seat.

As I lifted the rod, a solid weight was felt; no movement was evident, yet it appeared the line was cutting further upstream towards me. Winding down, I kept in touch with the unseen leviathan, but it did not show itself until it popped up, ready to be netted, and 15lb 9oz of barbel lay in the folds of the net - and yet again it was another occasion when I knew my eye was not on the action...

Sometimes the distraction is non-fishing-related; nowadays, this is more likely to be the ringing of your mobile phone. I feel a mobile can be a real pain; you go fishing to have peace and quiet, then the wife rings up to ask you a question... A few years ago, fishing within a couple of miles of home, I was slowly packing away as I had promised; my wife expected me home before 9.30pm - even though in June, daylight would last for at least an hour more.

Standing by the rod, still fishing, I was distracted by the mobile's screeching tone... Marie wanted to know that I was packing up, but before I had a chance to answer the call, the rod bucked in the rest and the reel went into overdrive. A long fight from an 11lb 12oz barbel ensured I would be late home;

fortunately, I had photographic evidence, and Marie was understanding.

So, are barbel psychic? A question which is light-hearted, as I do not really believe in the stuff; however, how often do we feel that sixth sense saying we should fish a certain swim, or even go fishing, knowing that something will happen? We leave our home in an unexplained positive mood; the journey to the swim is uninterrupted; the first cast is onto an invisible 'X marks the spot' in the swim; the atmosphere is so heavy and wired into the cosmic forces, the stars are all aligned - it is going to happen...!

The capture that made me question this came after a return to my favourite stretch after a break, during a session the day before, when, for nothing more than a change of scenery, I came to fish a stretch of the river that had not seen a bait of mine for over four years. The day had been pleasant, a slight downstream breeze and a hazy sky suggesting that the decision to fish was the right one. Starting to fish at the lower end of the backstream, two hours soon passed, and I sat soaking in the surroundings: the sound of birds calling, and dog-walkers in the nature reserve opposite calling out occasionally to get the dog back to heel.

In the early afternoon, I chose to move downstream onto the main river, to a swim that had always come good for me when I fished here regularly. I had only had a bait in the water a minute or so when the rod pulled round, resulting in a 12lb 12oz fish. This swim is very open, and can be observed by everyone walking the banks, so, deciding not to risk being seen, I moved as soon as the pictures were taken, returning to the backstream till dusk for one small chub.

That would have been enough, but the thrill I received left me wanting more; how was I to get fishing again when I had suggested to Marie that I would only fish on the Saturday...?

Sunday dawned expectant, charged with energy from that unknown, unseen force. It was impossible to not respond, yet the barrier of my promise to Marie appeared to be insurmountable.

However, I hoped it was nothing that gaining a few extra Brownie points could not fix. Marie wanted to go and see a friend in the morning, and I was roped into going with her - being the good husband that I am! However, I persuaded her to let me go down to the river instead, while she sat talking - I quickly drove the two miles to the river, and went for a walk where I had fished the day before. No one was in the swim; indeed, the whole stretch was devoid of anglers, so taking this as a good omen I hatched a plan that would hopefully get Marie to give me a pass later. Well, the plan did not work, yet I pleaded, I begged, and she eventually caved into my immaturity.

Leaving home at 2.00pm, excitement pumped adrenaline into my blood, and a rush of light-headedness swept through me. Normally, I don't suffer with road-rage, but today, every set of traffic lights was against me - eight sets across town, and not one was on green! Not one car in front of me was being driven by a boy racer - all were filled with Sunday OAP drivers! Arriving at the car park that usually has plenty of space, no room was available. What else could go wrong?

A journey that takes twenty minutes had taken twice that time; I didn't arrive in the swim till after 3.00pm, and at first things did not appear to improve. The hair was snapped on the set-up tackle... It took five casts to get a bait where I wanted it... By this time, I was questioning my sanity - had I misread my feelings? Had the stars unaligned that quickly? Eventually, after what seemed like an eternity, I felt reasonably comfortable, and settled in behind the rod to cool down with tea from the flask.

Before I left home, I had told Marie how I felt, and she had wished me well on the quest; as I resumed fishing, a quieter frame of mind began to arise again, slowly at first, a small, still voice reassuring me of the victory to be - with only two hours till dark, it would have to be soon, though...

Very rarely do I text Marie while fishing, knowing that if I do, she will reply, and a text conversation will begin. Today, however, feeling at peace, just after 4.00pm I started to compose a text: "Hi, sitting here quietly, still waiting for a.........". I never got to finish the text; I had taken my eye off the action, and now the reel was screaming at me as the rod was pulled off the front rest - the take was that violent.

Picking up the rod, a satisfying, heavy weight was felt, with little movement, yet the rod nodded to let me know a fish was attached. Slowly she moved upstream, occasionally giving a stronger pull and taking line off me, stopping me from becoming complacent. It wasn't till several minutes had passed that she turned anywhere near the water's surface. The boil suggested no more than a low double, and as she slipped into the net for the second attempt, I still didn't have a clue to her true size - only as I lifted the net, after allowing her to rest while I sorted out the scales and camera, did I really appreciate what was before me. As she left the water, the width of her belly looked awesome; the length of the body folded into the deep mesh of the 30-inch pan net gave the impression of an undersized net.

As I lifted the weigh-sling and scales, I had a guess of about 14lb already in my head, yet something inside was telling me it was more. Looking at the dial, it took me two glances to take the weight in - **A NEW PERSONAL BEST** of 15lb 15oz. Returning her to the net while I checked the positioning of the camera, I finished the text to Marie, telling her of my success and letting her know I would be coming home early. I didn't feel the need to have another cast; I had achieved my goal, and wished for no more, not wanting to dampen the euphoria bathing me. Pictures taken, I was walking away from the river by 4.30pm; amazingly, on both days no one walked past during either capture, no one saw me playing the fish, no one saw me weigh or photograph them... it was a dream of my own; no one else existed for those brief moments in time. Walking back to the car-park, I thought I felt a presence, a psychic power, a silent voice not heard or felt, yet calling ...

"TILL THE NEXT TIME, TAKE YOUR EYE OFF THE ACTION"

CHAPTER TWENTY-FIVE

A CHANGE IN FORTUNE – NO NEED TO LIE.

The ebb and flow of life provides a lack of consistency in all the activities undertaken in our daily passing of time. Angling is no different to any other pastime we use to fill the space through the twenty-four hours of each day. However, failing to keep a positive mindset may bring about a loss in our confidence to partake, and to achieve the results we wish to obtain.

Having chosen to not fish during what would be called the old close season for fishing - 15th March – 15th June - for the third year, 2017, an excitement was present on my first trip out. I felt a return to the stretch of water that had produced so well the previous year was called for, but a blank brought me back to earth with a bump. Why did I receive no action from the barbel in what I would describe as 'flier' swims? Was it the river being painfully low and clear compared to the season before - or had the angling gods forsaken me?

Every season since I first started fishing, I have kept a log of my fishing, recording weather and water conditions, number of hours fished (arrived and departure times), and tackle used – however, this has decreased and now disappeared from the logs - fish caught, position of swim they came from, and then a brief comment on the day. The purpose in my young mind when I started this was to see any pattern, rhyme, and reason for catching or not. I know many other anglers do this, and I suggest that for many of us it has shown that, inasmuch as we see a formula, we also see how unformulaic it really is. At times, the saying 'Disappearing up your own backside' comes to mind, as we try to fathom and look for logic in things we cannot control, such as the weather, and combine it with things we can - the bait and tackle we use; it is possibly the quickest route to confusion. When captures are not happening, yet everything we are doing is supposedly right, we may beat ourselves up and then question the positive rationale that has served us well in the past.

How many times do we implement a change because our bad results dictate it? Move to another river, change the bait we are using, even change some item of tackle that has served you well for decades... Several years ago, I fell into this trap in what now I consider to be a humorous way. The change came about during a short lull in captures from what has, through the years, been a very productive short stretch of river, and at a time when I needed to re-spool my reels. To my dismay, I hadn't checked on the amount of line left, and there wasn't even enough to spool one centrepin with fifty yards of it.

My preferred choice of line at that time - and now – was a fluorocarbon; however, another event affected my decision: the manufacturer of the line I used made a change to their product, as I discovered after a couple of unforced losses of fish due to knot-slips and unexplained breakages. I hunted out another line to replace it, and after trying two other fluorocarbons which didn't even make being spooled onto the reel, I did plenty of line testing and ended up with a monofilament line produced by Berkley called XTS - a line I have not seen for a while in any shop - given its abrasion resistance results, was it too good...?

Anyway, back to the story... The new line performed well, and I was satisfied that I had found a replacement; however, as already mentioned, the opportunity to purchase this line became rare a couple of years ago. I returned to fluorocarbon, and the 'improved' version of the line I used to use in the past. The first time out with the 'new' line, my confidence was sapped; something did not feel right. At first it was just a feeling, but it was a nagging, insurmountable feeling; it felt like a pain in my stomach, it was that strong. During the day, the direction of the sunlight changed and shaded the water in front of me; even the rippled, fast-flowing water could not hide the ugly vision I saw - the line looked as thick as a car tow-rope; this shouldn't be, as we are told fluorocarbon becomes invisible in water. I had never noticed it before, and it really set alarm bells ringing in my head.

The river I was fishing was gin-clear, and all the knowledge would suggest this wouldn't happen; the line was straight out of the packaging, and unused. It was only much further down the line (sic) that it was discovered that the 'improvement' made to this particular line had been to coat it in some way, thus rendering its fluorocarbon properties null and void. I did continue to use it for a very short period in varying conditions, and when used in an algae bloom it looked worse than in the clear stream.

While this was happening, my captures went from reasonable the season before to almost non-existent. I only landed three barbel, all about five pounds in weight, with another two lost, all season. At a loss, I wasted time, being indecisive and making mistakes; my confidence took a nose-dive - something had to be done to get catching again. What I have failed to say is that at the time of my original change, I had previously used another fluorocarbon line, one which, in my abrasion tests, had beaten all other lines out of sight; however, it had one failing, which I proved to be unfounded. This line had an overstated breaking strain, unlike other lines which are understated, eg: 'Sensor' 10lb normally breaks somewhere nearer 12lb; but this line, stated at 10lb, broke at under 9lb. To many anglers, this would ring alarm bells; however, after many years' angling my belief is that we should rely on the abrasion resistance.

In my tests, moving a line across a softwood fence-post, the same distance for each line, results varied drastically, 'Sensor' being one of the worst performers, snapping after as little as eight movements; however, the fluorocarbon would cut the wood and even lock up before snapping. Due to these findings, I fish on in the full knowledge that, if I can keep the fish moving without see-sawing too much, it will be landed from even the worse snag.

Even though it meant travelling thirty miles to the nearest stockist of the line, I knew it would be worth it in the end. The next season came upon me before I knew it. I used to work in Community Mental Health, and had been lucky enough to take clients/patients/users (still not sure what is politically correct...) fishing during the river close season, taking them to a carp puddle, women included, but I did not fish myself. The new line was put onto the reels, and instinctively I knew it was the line for me; there was no question that it would refract light or show up as badly with a build-up of algae - my mind-set was in the right place, and season 2014-15 proved this.

The season 2015-16, however, was a different kettle of fish; the decision was taken to fish a difficult stretch of the river, only just upstream from the previous one. Little was reported about this stretch, and I had the impression that it received very little angling pressure. Further upstream is a renowned stretch that has produced for those in the know for years. Results were not amazing; however, the end result had been on a par with my expectations. The highlight of the season, though, in January 2016, came as a real surprise; a change of scenery was required, and a visit to a stretch of river not visited for four years felt like a good idea.

Well, I have written over fourteen hundred words without really getting to the reason for this chapter's title; the change in fortune relates to the 2017-18 season. At the beginning of this season, I should have been on a high; however, during the two weeks of June I just could not get off the starting-block...

The first few trips only resulted in a high-single barbel and a lost fish; the latter really put the brakes on, having been hooked in a swim that had produced well at the same time last year. There appeared to be a new snag deposited under the willow, and this was the cause of concern. Any loss will niggle, and, if we allow it, sap our confidence. It did not help that the attention of the crayfish seemed more persistent than in previous years - the softer baits I preferred were being destroyed in minutes.

My mood was not helped with difficulties at work. Having changed jobs after seventeen years in Community Mental Health, due to the strain on my own health at the end of 2016, I had taken a job with the Ambulance service as a Patient Transport Driver, but the return to shift-work and the physical effort required had seen a loss of weight to nine and a half stone.

It was not until late October, when signed off work, that my mood started to improve; however, the improved catches in November were the catalyst that lit the fire of confidence once more.

A return to Kings Weir after a forty-three-year break

Thursday 16th November 2017

While signed off work with depression, it is very easy to fall into the trap of inactivity, and my wife constantly had to encourage me to keep going, applying for jobs and doing jobs around the house, with little thought of fishing.

Up to this point, I had fished less than one hundred and twenty hours all season, which equates to less than six hours a week. The majority of this time had been in the first six weeks, so many weeks had seen no fishing at all.

A couple of trips to fish the Hampshire Avon had been attempted, with no success, yet I felt a change is better than a rest, and decided a day on the River Lea at Kings Weir might bring a lift in my mood. I had not even seen the fishery for over forty-three years, so what made me decide on this trip is a bit of a mystery. A couple of conversations with a friend, Ray Kent, had lit the spark of interest, and he had invited me to join the Kings Weir Facebook group earlier in the season.

A telephone call to Ray, who fishes the weir regularly, made my mind up to make the horrendous journey around the M25; I felt that even if no fish came my way on the day, the return to childhood memories would lift my spirit. As the swims on the weirpool are bookable on a day-ticket, I took my friend's advice, and two days before made an advance selection of swim on his recommendation; feeling confident, plans were made for the trip.

Leaving home at 6.45am, hopefully early enough to get through the rush-hour or many hours of traffic on the M25 from Junction 15 to 26, I was surprised to encounter no hold-ups, and made the journey in a splendid one-and-a-half hours. Walking up to the lock-house to be greeted by Barbara, there was no rush to get to my chosen swim; no excitement either, though, just peace and calmness - a feeling I didn't recognise having on arriving at the river -however, it may happen more often than noticed, when everything comes together and the stars are aligned. I have felt it before and since, on the trips that have produced personal-best fish.

Unlocking the gate to the East bank of the weirpool opposite the house, I was greeted with an image that was not the same as I remembered from my youth; the flow and the positions of bankside trees had changed considerably.

I had booked swim EB1 against the weir-sill, and walking into the swim, I was happy to realise the use of heavy (2oz- plus) leads wouldn't be necessary to hold bottom; even the first cast under the sill held with a lead of 1½oz. This was the first rod, and a large piece of luncheon meat waited to be picked up by a barbel. The position of the second rod was a little more difficult to decide, so time was spent gently plumbing around with a small lead. After fifteen minutes of swinging the lead about, causing minimal disturbance by feathering it into the water, as is possible when casting with the centrepin, a spot I fancied was found. It was away from what were the obvious spots I had been told about, and the water was deeper by several feet than the surrounding areas.

Having brought a small amount (one pint) of hemp and casters with me, I felt this would be a good spot to drop about a dozen small droppers of bait - and even if a barbel didn't show, maybe a few smaller silver-fish might hold my interest through the day.

I set up with a one-ounce flat lead, a three-foot fluorocarbon hook-length, and a size 16 Pallatrax hook (these are nearer the size of a normal 12 - everyone thinks I'm mad using a size 16; however, I am not), hair-rigged with four casters for bait. I suppose this rod wasn't in situ until 9.45am, and sitting back, taking in the surroundings and remembering how noisy it can be fishing against a weir, I felt quietly and strangely confident.

What happened only thirty minutes later still took me by surprise; the old Gypsy d'Or centrepin reel went into overdrive on the caster rod, and had me lifting into an immensely powerful fish. The fight didn't really worry me, even though not being aware of the positions of snags in a new swim made me a little cautious. The fight took about five minutes before a massive barbel appeared at the net - I was taken aback; deep inside, I realised this was a fish of dreams, and a new personal best gazed up at me as she slid into the mesh.

I don't know why, but I called across to the angler opposite in WB1 and asked if he would come around to witness the fish. Letting her rest in the net, I slowly got the scales and camera ready while the angler came over. On the scales, the fish went 16lb 8oz - and I did lift her three times to make sure!

For the next two hours, I sat in a dream-like state, not really caring if another fish came my way. Ray had arrived just after the capture, and he suggested a walk along the members-only bank to give me an idea of the river downstream. We arrived back in the swim at 1.45pm, and the rods were quickly recast, with the caster rod over the droppered bait I had put down just before the walk.

Well, it must have been my day; as I sat down after putting the rod on the rests, the rod-tip started to knock in a manner unlike that caused by weed. I quickly decided to hit it, and the rod took on a satisfying battle-curve. A fight similar to the previous fish ensued, before another double-figure barbel hit the net. At 11lb 6oz, it was still a nice fish, and I wondered if the day could get any better.

The bait had only been back in the water for less than five minutes after the weighing and photographs when a slow take developed. Without realising it, I had called out to Ray again, as I had with the previous fish, and he was witness to a slow, deep fight. When the fish surfaced, we took stock of yet another double, and he commented that he would not be inviting me back for another visit... I hasten to say it was in jest - or at least I hoped so...!

We went through the weighing and photographic procedure, giving a weight of 12lb 15oz. We were amazed by this, and realised that the total weight of the three barbel was 40lb 13oz. No other barbel had been hooked on the pool during the day, and I felt as though I was an imposter who had come and stolen

the limelight that should have gone to another angler who fished the weir more often.

Return to normality?

It is surprising how quickly one good day will feed our id (ego, confidence); energy is channelled positively in how we present ourselves and complete our actions. Only three days later, a quick stolen trip to a local stretch of river with the remaining hemp and caster didn't produce any fish; although action was seen in the shape of two very heavy bends of the rod-tip, which didn't set the centrepin going. However, on retrieval soon after, the bait was missing on both occasions.

Not slow in coming forward, I returned three days later, and was prepared with more bait and four hours to fish. This trip produced a 4lb chub within minutes, quickly followed by a 12lb 12oz barbel, then a 10lb 8oz fish completed the day. Would I have made that trip to that swim if I had not made the captures in the previous few days? Unlikely, as it involved a walk of over a mile, and if my mood had been flat, I wouldn't have even thought about it, let alone done it.

At this point, be patient with me: a little detour of thought, a return to the first few paragraphs, and a question raised by the notes we keep. Earlier, I mentioned that I recorded the amount of time fished and in what conditions - I remember an article in 'Barbel Fisher': 'The Barbel Angler and Barbel River Compatibility Chart' by Tim Lennon. In it, he suggested a system of rating anglers on their experience and knowledge against the river's level of difficulty. This 'river rating' was based on the number of hours to barbel hooked/landed - this meant rod-hours, where, if using two rods, the hourly rate of sitting on the bank is halved: twenty hours becomes ten, and so on. Using his equation, only successful, experienced anglers should fish the hardest river, which meant over one hundred rod-hours per fish.

I get where he is coming from; however, a failing, which was not taken into account, in my opinion, is luck. My captures at Kings Weir may have been related to my skills as an angler;

however, would any other angler who had been in that swim on that day have caught those fish? Luck played a part in my being able to book the swim in the first place; it was evident that I was not confident in fishing the spots that I was told would produce, and it reared its ugly head when I went to the tackle shop to buy ONE PINT of caster - not enough to fish hemp and caster for barbel, we are told...!

Before anyone starts thinking that I am downplaying my catch, nothing is further from the truth; the reason for mentioning the statistics quoted by Tim gave is to question motive again. If we measure ourselves against other anglers' catch-rates, do we not lower our chances of catching? If I had fished that swim in a more negative fashion, I don't believe I would have caught either. Sometimes we need to relax; turn up, use the water skills we may have, and just fish - and stop punishing ourselves with failure. However, I acknowledge that I have fallen into the trap as much as the next man; we weigh ourselves against how good we are - is ours the biggest? Do I drive a better car than you? All this makes a man insecure, and drives us to become the best at what we do - but at what cost?

If I have managed to hold your attention thus far, the final destination for a change of fortune begins here. From November, my confidence stayed high, and even though I only fished a total of thirty hours over ten short afternoon trips, three chub and four barbel made their way into my net – however, it is one fish that I want to tell you about.

The New Year 2018 beckoned

Up until late December, the river had been running very low; it also had been affected by a high algae bloom all summer, that is until the autumn rains arrived in November, so the fish were not in the usual holding spots. If I had had the motivation, I should have gone searching; however, it was not until my recent captures that I felt positive enough to venture out more. The last week of December finally brought rain, and with a rising river I knew where to find the fish; as instinct led me to the swim, a still inner voice was encouraging me on. The thought was clear, and I almost felt I was being told the size of the fish I would catch... But not the first day - one was landed, at 12lb 9oz, yet it was not the one...

The next trip, on a Tuesday, was a blank, and I used it to spread a little loose-feed into the swim, preparing it for a trip planned for two days ahead. Between the days, rain continued to fall regularly; the river rose steadily, and it was just breaking the bank when Thursday arrived. Sitting down in the swim at 2.45pm, I only had till 5.00pm before leaving for home. I do not like night-fishing, and do believe that my captures have not suffered for not doing it; I can understand why many of you do it, but I like to see the rod go and watch the fight as well as feeling it. Within fifteen minutes the reel was screaming and the rod-tip bouncing, yet somehow I did not connect with it, but it only increased my confidence that I was in the right place.

The single bait was returned to the same piece of featureless water down below; I knew it was just upstream of an old weed-bed in a slight hole in the bottom gravel - this was the result of years of getting to know this stretch of river. I was aware that I was at peace, and a sense of confidence was rising that I only feel on days when something is going to happen - the still voice in my head of the days before came to calm me. No, I do not hear voices - I may suffer from depression, but have never had to worry about that...!

Anyway, it was 4.40pm, and I was tidying up the tackle and about to pour my last tea out of the flask when I received a slow take; only three clicks were heard from the centrepin, and the rod-tip hardly moved before I lifted into the fish. If first impressions are anything to go by, I would have thought the fish was a chub as it came towards the bank, a distance of about twenty feet, shaking its head and putting very little bend in the rod. Even when it started to bury into the bankside reeds, I still thought "chub"; however, this is when it all changed: from burying into the reeds, the fish took line at the pace of a tortoise (slight poetic licence), with the Harrison Torrix bent as far as it would go. Every movement could be felt, and the line was controlled by gently backwinding as the fish reached the far bank thirty-five feet away and bored away in the current.

It took about five minutes to bring her back to my bank, where she proceeded to bore away again, and it took several attempts to get her close enough to net. As she slipped into the landing net, I had difficulty getting her tail to drop in; I use a thirty-inch pan net, and this does not happen that often. Drawing the net to the bank to let her rest, her girth was immense; I was in a state of shock, and decided to rest the fish in the net while I packed away the few bits I had and then weigh and photograph her. It must have taken five minutes to pack away, and a further five minutes to set up the camera on a monopod, before I was even happy to bring her ashore.

Lifting the net by the frame, a weight was already in my mind, and she did not disappoint. Once unhooked and placed in the weigh-sling, I lifted her three separate times to settle on an honest weight. Here is another conundrum: why is it that some fish can look smaller in photos than others? I know there are many reasons for this - the size of the angler, distance held from the body, the size of aperture of the lens, the angle at which the picture is taken... It didn't help that by the time I was prepared to take the pictures darkness had fallen, and even though I used my standard settings and distances, I appeared to have made her look small. But is there a need to lie? Who am I deluding if I increase the weight of a fish - does it increase my standing with others? Of course it doesn't. When studying the pictures at home later, I was surprised how small she looked in the almost two-dimensional view; her width and shape did not really show how big she was.

After the last picture, and checking that they appeared fine, she was released gently back into her home. How big was she? I still haven't even given a clue as to the weight... All I will say is that she was heavier than the 16lb 8oz from Kings Weir earlier in the season, and was now my personal best (to be bettered in 2018).

CHAPTER TWENTY-SIX

DECEMBER DREAMS

Life can be a cruel master if we let it, throwing curve-balls, hitting us hard, just as we have picked ourselves up from the last difficulty. Posters advertising the film 'Jaws' in the 1970s expressed the feeling perfectly: 'Just when you thought it was safe to go back in the water...'. A world which deludes us that we can have everything we want, enjoy ourselves, and be always happy, kicks us in the teeth when a life-changing situation comes upon us, being unprepared for the emotions crashing over us like a tsunami wave to drown us.

Back in the summer of 2018, circumstances changed dramatically in my home life, and the life my wife and I led was turned on its head. Not to be too personal, there will be no mention of what caused this here; the changes are continuing, and are forever metamorphosing - however, we have emerged on the other side, stronger and resilient, and looking forward to a life full of hope.

By December of that year, we were recovering from the first part of the healing process, but just when we felt we were in a winning position, that curve-ball hit us for six. The day in question was Friday 21st December; our emotions were tearing us apart, yet we hung on in our faith and prayed for healing and strength.

Saturday dawned bright and clear, looking a perfect day to fish, which on getting out of bed was the last thing on my mind; however, Marie encouraged me to take a few hours out in the afternoon, to head down to the local river for a few hours' fishing.

Getting the tackle together and making a flask of tea took place in a state of trance; my mind was on other things, feeling that I should stay at home with Marie, but she would have none of it, so leaving the house at 11.45am, a journey uninterrupted by heavy traffic saw me arriving at the car-park ten minutes later.

Stepping out of the car, the warmness in the air was a surprise; a day in December that did not require a coat - it was left tucked into my chair until I was sitting in the swim. The walk was pleasant and short, the chosen swim being only three hundred yards down the river towards the road bridge.

Not wanting to sit in a swim that might not produce a fish, my first choice was one that I knew held fish at this time of year, next to a snag-tree. Most anglers fish this swim next to the tree; however, I will fish from a position fifteen yards upstream. If you had not plumbed this swim, it wouldn't be obvious that in the middle of nowhere, a gravel bar half the depth of the surrounding water gives a better chance of a feeding fish finding your bait safely. In summer, the bar is covered in weed, and by placing the bait close by, multiple catches had been made in previous years.

Slowly tackling up the already made-up rods, a pair of Harrison Torrix 1.75 test curve, Dave Swallow centrepin reels, 10lb X-line (fluorocarbon), and size 16 Pallatrax 'The Hook'. Where to cast was uppermost in my mind. I was on auto-pilot, still in a dream state, not really feeling I was there at all. Casting out by 12.30pm, I sat in a daze for twenty minutes or so before becoming aware of a sixth-sense thought bothering me, a quiet small voice; not a psychotic one - a voice of reason. An area in the swim I would never cast to – well, one that rarely saw my bait - called out for a bait to be cast there.

Fighting the prompting for five minutes, trying to fathom out why it was so strong, the right-hand rod was retrieved, and with a flick, the small fingernail-sized cube of luncheon meat was dropped into the spot with pin-point accuracy. A feeling of contentment came over me, relaxing in the unseasonable sun and warmth, and half an hour passed without disturbance.

As a user of centrepin reels, I still feel I will have a heart attack every time the reel goes into meltdown. Even the Dave Swallow being used, a relatively quiet reel, still makes a banshee-like howl as it screams off. So, when the first take came, to the bait placed in virgin territory, I jumped out of the chair with fright.

Expecting the fish to continue tearing off downstream, I was taken back as it held station before slowly plodding upstream towards my sitting position. This suggested a good fish, and after circling under the rod-tip for a few minutes, a mid-double barbel slid into the awaiting landing net. Weighing her at 14lb 10oz, my spirit was lifted; the circumstances at home were still the same, but a fish of this size eased the soul and helped clear the fog, at least a little.

A smile brightened my face; if nothing else was caught today, this fish had achieved its purpose. The time was still only 2.00pm, after weighing and photographing, and amazingly, no one went past on the footpath behind me in all the time from hooking the fish to completing the photos.

It is a very busy stretch of river; there are always people out for walks, heading to or from the town centre, or just out for a leisurely stroll. Trying to keep these swims from being overfished has always been a concern, and I only fished them less than ten times a season, even though I know I could catch more barbel if I fished more; it is better for the fish if they have an opportunity to rest. Unfortunately, since this day, the fishing appears to have declined, and over the seasons from 2019 to 2021 blanks became the norm.

Back to the day: with a bemused smile on my face, I sat for another forty minutes before the same rod screamed off once more. The battle followed the last, but one thing felt different: the weight pulsating up the line gave a magical essence, a fish of dreams, the fulfilment of the sixth sense that warmed me, telling me to cast to the unfished spot.

The fight lasted five minutes, not causing any concern; the fish behaved itself, the tackle proving its worth, and as the barbel surfaced I allowed a gasp of fresh air to be expelled from my mouth - the size was huge, and the depth of the fish was immense.

In the net, she lay quietly, while time was taken to prepare the camera and scales, all put within easy reach before bringing her ashore. The scales registered a new personal best of 17lb 9oz - a giant for the river she had come from. I had been unaware of the change in light conditions; sitting in a trance, no notice had been taken of the clouds rolling in and shading the sun. The day now had a wintery atmosphere, but the captures dispelled it - it still felt like summer to me.

However, to get a good photograph would require a flash to be used. After putting the camera on the tripod, a few test shots were taken, and showed that I had a problem. The battery in the flash was dead; the spare had been in the bag too long had no power either. Juggling the settings on the camera to achieve a good shot became impossible as the light levels dropped even further – so any shot would have to do. Disappointed not to have a good picture, I acknowledged that she will live in the mind's hard-drive until my memory fades, and packed up early. Having started to fish at 12.15pm, only two-and-a-half hours later, at 3.45pm, I was walking on air back to the car, and with a lifted spirit, I returned home to support Marie and continue to fight the good fight.

Before that day, I had only caught one other barbel in December, and that was the previous season from the same swim. December had always been a bogey month as far as barbel were concerned. Nothing had changed in the way I fished, so why they started to end up in my landing net had me confused, yet happy. To complete the month, the following Saturday, another three-hour session produced two more fish, both doubles.

These didn't come from the same area of the swim as the two the week before; both were caught off a mid-river spot near the bar. Like peas in a pod, they weighed 12lb 14oz and 12lb 15oz.

Like other fish, barbel do not always play by the rules, following our expectations of what we think they will do. If you read all the books or articles concerning catching barbel, everyone will say that the bite you will receive is a 'three-foot twitch'. The first two had both screamed off at a rate of knots, but these two gave no more than a couple of clicks on the centrepin and a knocking rod-tip.

Forward two years, to December 2020 - life has found an even keel again. Any difficulties Marie and I have endured through the last two years have been resolved, and we are able to look forward to a bright future. Our life balance restored, we are both smiling; however, still learning to compromise, to give space to each other to develop our skills and take time to recharge our batteries.

The last chapter in the book is, for me, the most important - even though angling plays only a small part in it. Faith is a part of me; it enables me to accept myself and others. Hopefully, you will continue to read.

CHAPTER TWENTY -SEVEN

THE MISSING YEARS

Time is a continuum, flowing in a straight line: beginning, middle, and end; past, present, and future; the motion of passage through a life is finite. If the learning process of maturity is seen in a similar way, lessons and mistakes made would become fewer as we learn more, yet experience proves otherwise. An ebb and flow goes through our life, backwards and forwards, never finishing until our last breath.

The life led from childhood to adulthood had been an attempt to drown the lack of self-belief within myself. As with many children from broken homes, I blamed myself for the break-up of my parents' marriage; I believed I was unlovable and caused all their problems, which as an adult I learnt was untrue. The hard shell I created, doused in drink and drugs, failed to protect; the shell had made it worse. There was no label on my feelings or behaviour; only a decade later, after seeing a doctor, did I call it depression.

When I returned home from the summer of 1979 working at Butlin's, fishing still enabled me to escape and forget my feelings and emotions. Sitting on the river-bank or lake-side, everything can be forgotten; man loses himself in a world of his own – sometimes, though, even being out on the bank doesn't stop the thoughts invading the inward space of his life.

Something was missing; relationships had been attempted – unsuccessfully; progression in employment had hit a proverbial brick wall, and angling was not cutting it as an escape, either. Drink became a hideaway of choice. Fortunately, I had weaned myself off drugs - one good decision, made with the realisation that the only person I was hurting was myself. While taking the illegal substances, the belief that I was getting back at loveless relationships and the world gave me excuses that now are seen as empty.

A hole existed in my soul; not knowing what would fill it, a search began, ironically in the past. It had been seven years since contact had been made with my natural father; memories of a weak man crying in the spare bedroom on the night he left home had clouded the image of someone who, however bad, should still mean something in my life.

The address in an address book; a phone number unused, dialled with trepidation; waiting for a voice to say hello... Fear gripped; the wait dragged and dived into the abyss. Finally, the sound of the receiver being lifted raised the heartbeat further, before the baritone voice of my father said "Hello?". The conversation, remembered vaguely, did not last too long, but it didn't leave a terrible taste in the mouth, either. We agreed to meet up at the weekend, at the local Little Chef.

When the weekend came, time had flown by; there hadn't been anything else on my mind - work and fishing and life at home took a back seat. There had been no mention to my mum and stepdad that I had arranged to meet Michael, my father; I believed there would be an explosive discussion when they did find out.

Waiting in the car-park, I wondered if the right decision had been made, but the chance to run was lost, as he had arrived. The greeting, laboured and reserved, felt uncomfortable, but as time went on, after a cup of tea or two, an ease fell on the conversation. An hour passed, and I wanted to return home to give myself space to analyse the thoughts bombarding my mind.

From this meeting grew a need to renew my relationship with Michael. By 1981, having passed my driving test, almost every weekend I would drive to visit him, his wife and her three children, staying overnight, which became another way of running from my insecurities.

Michael had been a Walter Mitty (a fictional character, who lived in a dream world of fantasy) when he lived with the family, up to twelve years before, trying to be something he was not. Through the years, even though still present, it had diminished; he lived a quiet life in a small Suffolk village - however, he still wanted to be involved in everything.

Meeting his wife in 1980, there had been a change that I found baffling. Looking for a church to be blessed in, he had started a friendship with a local Pastor, through which my father had made his profession to become a Christian. Knowing him, as I thought, this appeared to be a difficult thing for him, and for the first couple of years I saw little change in his behaviour; there was still an acting-out of frustration and anger that, from how I perceived being a Christian, made it untrue, yet I continued to visit and stay for weekends.

Every Sunday, as Michael and his wife left for a church service, they would ask me if I wished to join them, but every time I would say no, burying my head back under the bed-covers to recover from the hangover that drinking on Saturday night had lumbered me with. Every Sunday for three years, almost Groundhog Day-like, the same routine was followed - each time the same answers and actions.

Sunday 4th April 1984

What was different, I will never know, but ten seconds before Michael and his wife walked through the door on their way to church, I changed my mind and shouted for them to wait.

The walk through the small chapel doors, a sense of "what am I doing here?" arose, questioning the very fact of being there; wanting to turn straight back out again, but believing it would be a loss of face, I continued taking the few steps to the pew at the back. Michael and his wife continued further into the church, leaving me with my thoughts.

The congregation was no larger than thirty, mainly husbands and wives with young children in tow. No one said hello, all intent on preparing themselves for the forthcoming hour. The service passed in a blur; I have no memory of the songs sung, the prayers, the sermon... all disappeared beneath my thoughts.

But before I got out of the pew, the realisation that I felt different warmed my being. A heaviness had lifted; a smile upon my face must have been observed by the people around me. Standing at the door, the Pastor struck up a conversation, and before I knew it, I had invited myself to go and see him later in the day.

That week, instead of just staying overnight, I was with Michael until Thursday. I found myself visiting the Pastor every day, undertaking studies of the bible over food prepared by his wife.

The change in my life was not immediate; the need to stay in the comfort of my insecurities and lack of self-belief tugged at me; the "better the devil you know" syndrome tempted me to seek satisfaction, to drink myself under the table, and the solitary life at the waterside appeared to be an easier option.

However, the best path is not always the easy path. Staying in a place where growth is impossible, where eyes are shut and emotions not dealt with, leads to a deeper depression; without a faith, man is like a ship without a mast or rudder, being pushed aimlessly in a life with no purpose.

The choice of faith in God had not been my first choice; I had read many books on other beliefs; I had tried mind-altering drugs, being a football fan, and angling, too. All are, in themselves, empty, hollow mantras saying nothing to me. For a faith to be a positive influence on man, it needs to fill a need within us. All beliefs give a sense of belonging, and most importantly meet the need to be loved.

If a faith gives you both, belonging and love, it is a positive attribute in a life. I would not belittle or criticise anyone for their different belief, nor would I not push mine upon them, while, however, believing the one chosen is the right one for me.

We are not to judge others; there is a love called 'Agape', the love of unconditionality, loving someone for who they are, not for what they do. I may not like what you do as a sport, or how you live your life; however, I will still love you for who you are.

Keeping a faith is difficult. For the first two years, my faith enabled me to grow as a person, and led into the profession of Social Services, working with homeless adolescents, leading to nearly twenty years in the community with individuals suffering with mental health difficulties.

Angling took a back seat, with me having found another purpose that gave peace and lifted the depression, but the breakdown in my health in 1988 soon dragged me back into the quicksand of despair. For three years, a return to drinking heavily, and fishing full-time, except for work, I self-neglected unintentionally. Working as a milkman, I would get out of bed at 3.00am, finish the round by 10.00am at the latest, return home, pick up the fishing tackle and drive straight down to the lake. Little food was consumed while fishing or at home; a morning fry-up at the cafe on the round and a couple of pints of milk off the float sufficed.

Getting home after dark, summer or wintertime, bathing would be a quick cat's-lick of a wash, a beer or three before bedtime at midnight or later, and the next day would start all over the same.

If I had any friends, socialising was not happening, because of the fishing and my personal hygiene. This compounded the negative persona that had fallen over me once more. Losing my job in 1991, even more time was spent at the lakes - something had to change. In the backwoods of the mind, the belief seen in 1984 kept prompting and calling out to be rekindled.

One dark evening in winter found me sitting on the bank at Broadacres, when a quiet voice beckoned, encouraging me to pack up and go to church; fighting it, I finally gave in. Packing up, the walk past the other three pits was a struggle, the drive home hampered by a car that did not want to start. Arriving home, I slowly had a wash, changed into 'slightly' cleaner clothes, and left the house for a church half a mile away.

Walking up the road in the dark coldness, I tried to dissuade myself, convincing myself that if the lights were not on in the church, it meant I was not meant to attend! Turning the corner on which the church stood, I noticed the light in the porch was off; almost gladly, I started to turn towards home - but amazingly, a light glowed from out of the church door as someone opened it from the inside.

Was it that I had just arrived at the right time, or was it a God incidence, or a coincidence? Believe whatever you will, I went into the church, and through fellow believers and my belief in God, the struggle to rebuild my life arose again.

Some say that difficulties make us stronger; I could not agree more. Through the twists and turns of life, a balance is constantly in flux. From my faith, the balance of family life, fishing and faith have continued to encroach upon each other, yet it becomes easier and more fulfilling as time goes by.

Life has been full of obsession; depression even created its own. A balance needs to be found by us all - angling as part of a complete life, healthier than as a stand-alone element of the whole.

So, are we at the end of the story? Nothing is over until it is over. Life continues to throw lessons at us all until we pass into physical death and our life on earth is finished; this is not goodbye. Till we next meet.

Lightning Source UK Ltd.
Milton Keynes UK
UKHW020747140721
387104UK00004B/199/J

9 781839 756498